Chocolate
Never Faileth

Chocolate
Never Faileth

More Than 125 Heavenly Recipes

Recipes by *Annette Lyon*

Table of Contents

Important Notes on Non-Chocolate Ingredients

Please read through this section, because every time I list an ingredient in a recipe, I won't repeat these explanations. They're all in this section, and they're all important. The same goes for the sections on melting, storing, and measuring chocolate. All of it is important information you'll need throughout your chocolate journeys, but repeating it in each recipe would get annoyingly redundant.

BUTTER

When working with chocolate, make sure—unless otherwise stated—the butter is softened and at room temperature before you use it. If it's too cold or too warm, it won't mix into the recipe properly, and its temperature might even affect the chocolate or cocoa. Unless otherwise stated, every recipe in this book uses salted butter. I know that most professionals use unsalted butter. But I'm not a professional, so I use what's already in the house: salted butter. Though I had to make some tweaks, all the recipes in this book will turn out just fine with salted butter. If you want to use unsalted butter, you'll need to add a quarter teaspoon of salt to compensate.

MELTED BUTTER

Some recipes require melted butter instead of softened butter. The recipe may specify that you let the melted butter cool a little before adding it. I cool mine more quickly by putting it into the freezer or fridge for about five minutes. This way, the butter stays melted but is not hot enough to upset the temperamental nature of the cocoa. (You think hormonal women are moody? You haven't seen anything until you've tried working with cocoa.)

WHIPPING CREAM AND WHIPPED CREAM

When I refer to whipping cream, I mean the liquid cream you get in the dairy case and whip in a bowl with beaters. I always mean heavy whipping cream, not half-and-half or any other variety. If you're not familiar with how to whip cream, don't worry; it's not hard. Use beaters and a bowl and beat the cream on high speed. Whip it long enough to make it fluffy and stiff, but not long enough that it starts turning into butter. I like to sweeten whipping cream with powdered sugar because it dissolves nicely and adds a soft sweetness that also holds up the fluff.

1

You can also add up to a teaspoon of vanilla extract for added flavor if you like. If you use them, beat the powdered sugar and/or vanilla into the cream last thing, at low speed. The whipping process tends to go faster and make fluffier cream if you put the bowl and beaters into the freezer for half an hour before using them. It's a nice step if you're thinking ahead, but it's not a necessary one. I can't vouch for how well any of these recipes will turn out if you use Cool Whip or some other fake whipped topping in place of real whipping cream. Do it at your own risk—and then never, ever tell me about it, because I won't be your friend.

Whipped cream refers to cream that has already been whipped and is no longer liquid. You might have whipped it yourself, or you might have purchased it in a can. Whipped cream in cans is real cream, so I consider it perfectly acceptable to use for garnish, but it cannot be substituted for whipped cream in recipes.

PEANUT BUTTER
Any recipe calling for peanut butter refers to creamy peanut butter, not chunky. The peanut butter needs to melt and incorporate with the chocolate, and that can't happen if it contains chunks of peanuts.

I prefer to use natural peanut butter, which means it doesn't have sugar, trans fats, and other things added to it (ingredients that allow you to put your peanut butter on the shelf instead of in the fridge). The oils in natural peanut butters separate after you mix them; to keep the oils mixed, the peanut butter has to be refrigerated. Even though I prefer "real" foods, some of the recipes (such as Tiger Bites) might hold up better at room temperature if you use regular peanut butter. Natural-oil peanut butters are softer at room temperature, so if you use natural-oil peanut butter you might need to keep things like Tiger Bites in the fridge to maintain their shape and texture.

COFFEE CREAMERS
Several recipes use powdered flavorings—coffee creamers, such as Coffee-Mate®—that are used to flavor coffee. These are often available in liquid form in the dairy section, though my recipes specify using them in powdered form (the powders are usually found on the coffee aisle). Rest assured that these contain no coffee, so you can use them without any Word of Wisdom concerns. Coffee creamers are simply flavorings

that add a really nice creamy flavor to certain recipes. Hazelnut is my favorite, but I've also seen caramel, cinnamon, and vanilla. Yum!

FLAVORED SYRUPS AND EXTRACTS

I'm a huge fan of vanilla extract—just make sure it's real vanilla extract and not vanilla flavoring. When someone gives me a recipe calling for two teaspoons or even a tablespoon of vanilla, I know I've found a friend. Other flavors and extracts complement chocolate as much as or even more than vanilla. I love to add almond extract to chocolate recipes; orange and mint extracts are also excellent with chocolate.

You can also experiment with various flavored syrups—liquid flavorings that work well in drinks and ice creams, but that are less concentrated than extracts. Syrups are available at the grocery store, often near coffee creamers and hot cocoas.

NON-GROCERY-STORE ITEMS

This book has just a few recipes that require ingredients not found at a typical grocery store. For example, the chocolate extract or chocolate flavoring for Chocolate-Scented Play Dough may be difficult to find in a regular grocery store; you may need to buy it online or at a confectioner's shop. Whenever there is an ingredient like that, I note it in the recipe.

DRY VAN/DRY VANILLA

One unusual ingredient I use in a few recipes is Dry Van, a powdered form of vanilla; it's available online or at specialty cooking stores. The only recipes that call for it are those that result in a dry product (which is why you can't use vanilla extract). In each recipe, you could probably get away with leaving out the powdered vanilla—but, of course, vanilla always adds that little extra something. The recipes call for only a little Dry Van, so if you ever buy any, it should last you just this side of eternity.

COCONUT OIL

Some grocery stores have health-food sections, but your best bet for finding coconut oil is at your local health-food store in the cooking oil section. Only a few of the recipes in this book call for it, but I do recommend having some on hand. It's great for cooking cakes, and it's critical for Magic Shell for Ice Cream—which you have to make if you have kids, grandkids, nieces, or nephews . . . or contact with children in any way, shape, or form. It's even necessary if you have a child hidden somewhere inside you. Note for women: Coconut oil is also great for the skin, and it's a fantastic eye makeup remover, especially for waterproof mascara. As you rub it into the mascara, you're moisturizing the skin around your eyes!

EGGS AND EGG WHITES

All eggs in these recipes are meant to be large eggs. The size is very important to the recipe. For most recipes, let the eggs sit at room temperature for ten or fifteen minutes instead of using very cold eggs straight from the fridge; the recipes turn out a little better. This is particularly true of egg whites. The warmer the eggs when you separate them, the better—the whites will beat fluffier and faster.

Also note that when beating egg whites, the bowl must be free from all traces of water and grease. It's not going overboard to wash the bowl and the beaters twice and dry them with a dish towel and then a paper towel.

LECITHIN AND NONSTICK SPRAY

Chocolate chips (especially white chocolate chips) are made to hold their shape when cooked, such as with chocolate chip cookies; generally, they're designed not to melt. In some of these recipes, you'll be purposely melting them and doing other things with them. That means you'll need to gently encourage the chips to let go of their shape and thin up a bit.

Since the two main ingredients of chocolate are cocoa and cocoa butter, the best way to thin chocolate chips is to add a bit of oil to them as they melt. Often a teaspoon of vegetable oil will do the job. Lecithin also works wonders, if you have it on hand. I'm betting you do have lecithin in your house and just don't know it. Ever use nonstick cooking spray? Guess what one of the main ingredients is? Lecithin. The other main ingredient is usually canola oil. Between the two, they create a great nonstick surface. They also create a fantastic thinning agent for chocolate chips—without measuring spoons or any mess. If you're melting chocolate and it needs just a little thinning, grab your nonstick spray and give the chocolate a two- to three-second squirt, then stir. It'll probably do the trick.

Despite its therapeutic value, note that chocolate is not deductible as a medical expense.

Important Chocolate Information

I love chocolate, but the more I've worked with it, the more I've developed a love/hate relationship with it. Why? I've learned just how temperamental the stuff can be. If you get it just a little too hot, it seizes, turning into a hard, gross mass that might as well be a chocolate rock. If you don't treat cocoa just right, the entire cake falls. What follows is valuable information you need to know before you work with chocolate. I learned a lot of it the hard way, but you don't have to. And a lot of it is simple—once you know it. The information here is relevant to nearly every recipe in this book. You'll need to know this stuff. READ IT. Skip it, and you'll regret it. Read it, and you'll thank me.

COCOA
Every recipe in this book that calls for cocoa requires regular, unsweetened cocoa. Do not use Dutch-processed cocoa. Dutch-processed cocoa is more alkaline, so the cocoa has a softer flavor. But when you're baking, chemistry is everything; if you alter the pH of chocolate, the recipe won't turn out the same.

BUYING BAKING CHOCOLATE
When using baking chocolate, read the label carefully to determine how much each square weighs. Here's why: a recipe may tell you to use "two squares (two ounces)." One square of baking chocolate might be one ounce—but an entire big chocolate bar might be four ounces, meaning that each of its eight squares is only half an ounce.

The four-ounce bars with the half-ounce squares melt well and taste good; I use them all the time. Just remember that their "squares" weigh half of what the typical "square" of chocolate does, so you'll need to double the number of squares to get the right amount of chocolate.

MELTING CHOCOLATE: THE BASICS
You must treat melted chocolate the way it wants to be treated, or it will bite back. In other words, you must learn how to temper it (a very appropriate term, considering how volatile the stuff is.)

Here are a few of basic do's and don'ts:

—Use a glass or earthenware container for even heat distribution and retention; if melting chocolate in the microwave, make sure the container is microwave safe. I prefer to use a Pyrex bowl for melting in the microwave.

—If you're using baking chocolate or other chocolate that's in bigger pieces, break the chocolate into small pieces before melting. A knife acts as a great wedge to break off chunks. If you're using chocolate chips, simply dump them into the bowl.

—No matter how you melt your chocolate, don't cook it too long or at too high a temperature, or the chocolate will seize or scorch—turning the chocolate into a hard, grainy mass. You can't fix seized chocolate. It's ruined, because the molecules have been destroyed. All you can do at that point is mourn the loss, throw it out, and start over.

—Stir the melting chocolate frequently. This helps temper the chocolate so it develops a beautiful chocolate sheen as it cools and hardens. It also allows oxygen to get into the chocolate, lowering the temperature so it won't bloom as it cools. (See "What's That White Stuff on My Chocolate? Or: Chocolate Bloom," p. 8.) If melted chocolate feels remotely too hot to the touch, it's too hot. Stir it and stir it some more. It should feel just slightly cooler than body temperature. This is most important for projects where the hardened chocolate is the focus, such as Chocolate Bark.

HERE ARE THE VARIOUS TECHNIQUES FOR MELTING CHOCOLATE:

THE OVEN METHOD
Set the oven lower than 180 degrees. You should be able to take the bowl out of the oven with your bare hands; if you can't, it's too hot. Stir the chocolate occasionally with a wooden spoon to help smooth lumps. If there are a few lumps when you remove it from the oven, simply let the bowl sit, stirring the chocolate every few minutes; the heat in the melted chocolate will melt the rest of the lumps.

THE MICROWAVE METHOD
Melt the chocolate a microwave-safe bowl for forty-five to sixty seconds, then stir with a rubber scraper. After that, cook at twenty- to thirty-second intervals, stirring between each. When there are just a few small lumps left, stop cooking; let the chocolate sit. The remaining heat in the bowl and the chocolate will melt any remaining lumps, and you'll be able to stir it smooth within a minute or two.

THE DOUBLE-BOILER METHOD

If you don't have an actual double-boiler to use, boil water in a medium-sized pan. Place the chocolate in a smaller pot or a bowl that won't fall into the water, and place the smaller pot or bowl over the boiling water. Stir to melt. This method keeps the heat a step away from the chocolate.

THE FRYING PAN METHOD

Put the chocolate pieces into a heavy frying pan and set the burner to low. Let the chocolate melt, stirring periodically. When the chocolate is mostly melted, turn off the burner and let the remaining heat melt the rest of the chocolate. I have personally had the least success with this method—possibly because I'm just impatient, and this method seems to take the longest.

THE ZIP-BAG TRICK (Shhh! Even the pros use it!)

You've surely seen fancy chocolate drizzles—like the ones on chocolate-dipped strawberries or over cakes, éclairs, and even cookies. You probably assumed that whoever made them had a virtual baker's toolkit to achieve such beautiful results—or, at the very least, a fancy, professional icing bag.

Hah!

Chances are, the pro used a plastic zip-style bag, available at your friendly neighborhood grocery store. It's simple! Even my youngest did it all the time when she was in preschool. The trick is to use zip-style resealable freezer bags. Freezer bags are thicker than regular bags, so they better handle the pressure as you squeeze the chocolate out (no oozing from burst seams). They also allow you to aim better.

Here's how it works: Put your hand inside the zip-bag to open it up. With one corner facing down, set the bag all the way inside a tall, wide, drinking cup. This frees up both of your hands and holds the bag in just the right position for filling. Fold the edges down over the sides of the cup.

Spoon/pour the melted chocolate (or cream puff filling, pudding, or other substance) into the bag. When the bag is full, let out most of the air and then zip up the bag.

Use a pair of sharp scissors (high-tech tool!) to snip off a corner of the bag. In most cases, the hole should be no more than the size of a pencil lead, but for some projects—such as cream puffs or éclairs—it'll need to be bigger. Appropriate instructions are in each recipe.

Voila! You have your own piping bag. Use the bag to drizzle chocolate over whatever dessert you've created—with perfect control. When the bag is empty, simply throw it out—along with the mess inside. (Note: This kind of drizzle bag works particularly well for squeezing leftover chocolate into kids' mouths.)

STORING CHOCOLATE—ASSUMING SOME IS LEFT OVER

Nothing is worse than putting a piece of chocolate in your mouth, anticipating a sweet indulgence, but getting melt-in-your mouth garlic and onion flavors instead.

Trust me—I've done it. Not pretty.

The worst chocolate I've ever had was a pack of M&Ms that had been shipped across the ocean via ship. The M&Ms spent weeks, if not months, absorbing the smell of the cardboard and shampoo they were snuggled against.

To avoid such nasty encounters, store your chocolate in an airtight container in a place with no funky odors, flavors, perfumes, cleaners, or anything else that could be absorbed and affect flavor.

Regular zip-style plastic bags can work in a pinch for brief storage stints, but they generally aren't thick enough to keep out strong odors like spices. If you have to use them, double up. Freezer bags are better because they're thicker (and can keep out odors longer).

Your best bet is a plastic container with a secure lid. Even then, store the chocolate next to safe items that don't have strong smells or flavors. Airtight containers are also important because condensation can ruin chocolate, making it bloom (more about that below).

In the right environment, chocolate can be safely stored for years. One professional says he stores his chocolate next to his olive oil because they have the same storage requirements: a cool, dry place.

Avoid storing chocolate on an outside wall of your house, since outside walls have greater temperature fluctuations. Even when insulated, an outside wall is warmer than the rest of the room in summer and cooler in winter.

Some chocolate pros say you can store your chocolate in the freezer, but that poses a risk of condensation (and blooming) when it warms back up. To avoid bloom, try to keep any chocolate temperature changes gradual. For example, transfer it from the freezer to the fridge for a day. Then transfer the chocolate from the fridge to the coolest room of the house to let it warm up for a day before you use it.

WHAT'S THAT WHITE STUFF ON MY CHOCOLATE? OR: CHOCOLATE BLOOM

Bloom is that unsightly whitish/gray coloring on the surface of chocolate. Blooming occurs when the fat and/or sugar particles in the chocolate separate from the rest of the chocolate and migrate to the surface. Chocolate bloom is generally caused by condensation on the surface, rapid temperature changes (which can also cause condensation), or poor tempering. Bloom doesn't always affect flavor (although it can), but it often affects the texture of the chocolate. Bloomed chocolate is perfectly safe to eat, but it doesn't look—and won't taste—as good. You can usually cook with bloomed chocolate, and it sometimes hides well inside a recipe.

MEASURING CHOCOLATE

Most of the recipes in this book use easy measurements: either ounces of baking chocolate, measuring cups' worth of cocoa, or measuring cups' worth of chocolate chips.

Here are a few suggestions:

—A typical bag of chocolate chips holds roughly 2 cups. Since I tend to buy larger bags, I actually measure out 1 cup at a time and call it 8 ounces, but the recipes won't be ruined if you use half a bag when a recipe calls for slightly more.

—My favorite milk chocolate chips are in the silver Guittard bag. They are jumbo-sized, which means that when you measure them, they may actually come to one cup, but they have more air between the chips, so they don't melt down to quite the same amount. Any time you're using a larger chip or chunk, remember that the air spaces will affect the melted measure.

—It's worth investing in an inexpensive postal scale for measuring ounces of chocolate. They're small, cheap, easy to use, and very much worth the trouble, especially if you use fancier chocolates instead of grocery-store products.

Just a few tips: Chocolate often comes packaged by weight (one-pound bags, five-pound bags, and so on), so that alone can get you on the right track in guessing roughly how much to use even without a postal scale.

As a basic rule of thumb, 1 cup of chocolate chips or Guittard A'Peels = 6 ounces of chocolate = about ⅔ cup of melted chocolate. Remember: these amounts are approximate and should be considered as guidelines. The actual quantity varies, depending on the shape and size of the unmelted pieces you're using.

Note: One cup of chocolate chips equals six ounces of any other kind of chocolate. However, you can increase it to a heaping cup, making it a full half pound or eight ounces if desired.

KEEPING CHOCOLATE WARM AND MELTED WHILE WORKING

If you're working on a large project, melted chocolate may set before you want it to, regardless of the method you used to melt it. Following are some of my favorite no-fail ways of keeping chocolate at the right temperature until you've finished the project.

9

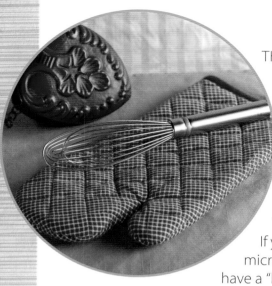

THE SLOW-COOKER

Plug in a slow-cooker on low. Put a little water and a washcloth in the bottom. Then place your chocolate-filled container inside, and the chocolate will stay perfectly melted.

THE OVEN

Keep Pyrex bowls of chocolate in an oven at no higher than 180 degrees. Make sure you can handle the bowls with your bare hands.

THE MICROWAVE

If your microwave has a "hold warm" setting, periodically put the chocolate into the microwave and cook your chocolate for a few minutes on that setting. If you don't have a "hold warm" setting, cook it at half power for a minute or so.

THE ELECTRIC HEATING PAD

Plug in an electric heating pad on high, cover the pad with a dishcloth (to prevent staining the pad), and place chocolate-filled zip-style freezer bags, bottles, bowls, or any other container on top of the heating pad.

GETTING DARING?

Once you've experimented with these recipes, you may want to bump your efforts up a notch by trying fancier chocolates and cocoas. The resources section lists various types of ingredients and where to look for them.

10

Cakes

No chocolate cookbook would be complete without a Devil's food cake recipe. This is my version of an old classic. It's dense, it's rich, and it's delicious. You can use it as a two-layer cake using 8-inch rounds or bake it in a 9 x 13 glass dish. Either way, it's downright sinful, just like it's supposed to be. Don't skip the step of mixing the cocoa into the boiling water. There's a good reason for it: the boiling water releases the strongest possible chocolate flavor from the cocoa, giving the cake the strongest possible flavor—something all chocoholics look for.

Devil's Food Cake

1⅓ C. WATER

¾ C. COCOA

1¾ C. SUGAR

1 STICK BUTTER

1 TSP. VANILLA

2 EGGS

¼ TSP. SALT

1½ TSP. BAKING SODA

2¼ C. FLOUR

PREHEAT OVEN TO 350. Grease and lightly flour two 8-inch round pans; put a round piece of waxed paper in the bottom of each pan, and grease the waxed paper as well. As an alternate, grease a 9 x 13 baking dish. In a small saucepan, boil the water. Add the cocoa and mix well. Remove from heat and set aside. In a mixing bowl, cream the sugar, butter, and vanilla until light and fluffy. Add the eggs one at a time, mixing a full minute between each egg. Pour in about half of the cocoa mixture, careful not to splash, and mix it in. Scrape the sides of the bowl as necessary. Add the salt and baking soda and mix. Add the flour and combine well. Add the last of the cocoa mixture, again scraping the sides of the bowl, and mix until just combined. Don't over-mix, or the cake can become tough. Pour the batter into the prepared pans. Bake 8-inch rounds for 35–40 minutes or a 9 x 13 dish for 40–45 minutes, until a toothpick inserted in the center comes out clean. When checking for doneness, be careful not to slam the oven door, or the cake will fall in the center. Cool on a wire rack. Ice as desired.

Don't let the name fool you; this one isn't exactly healthy. The taste is more of a cross between Devil's Food Cake and a thick brownie. No matter how you look at it, the cake's enough to put you into a chocolate coma. (Even my daughter who despises oatmeal can't get enough of it.) Since the cake tends to bake more flat than domed, it's particularly easy to ice, so you have no excuse not to. Just do it when the cake is totally cooled so you don't have oodles of crumbs rolling themselves into the icing.

Chocolate Oatmeal Cake

1½ C. OATMEAL

1½ C. WATER

1½ STICKS BUTTER, MELTED AND COOLED IN THE FRIDGE FOR ABOUT 5 MINUTES

2 C. SUGAR

2 EGGS

2 TSP. VANILLA

1 TSP. SALT

¾ C. COCOA

2 TSP. BAKING SODA

1 TSP. BAKING POWDER

2½ C. FLOUR

PREHEAT OVEN TO 350. Coat a 9 x 13 pan with nonstick spray. In a small bowl, soak the oatmeal in the water (this is good to do while the melted butter is cooling.) Meanwhile, cream the butter and sugar together until fluffy. Add the eggs and vanilla. Add the salt, cocoa, baking soda, baking powder, and flour, and mix well. Add the oatmeal and water mixture; blend well and pour into the pan. Bake for about 35 minutes. Cool and top with your favorite chocolate icing. Tip: This batter is quite thick, so while a hand-held beater can manage in a pinch—groaning and complaining at you along the way—you might want to use a stand-alone mixer to make things easier.

I have many fond memories from my childhood of watching Mom and Dad make Cockeyed Cake; it was the go-to dessert when we wanted something fun, easy, and (most importantly) chocolaty. Mom and Dad liked to make a "nest" in the dry ingredients for each wet ingredient before mixing them all up. This recipe is so simple because you mix it in the baking pan itself—no mixing bowl or beaters to wash!

Cockeyed Cake

1½ C. FLOUR (SEE NOTE #1)

3 TBSP. COCOA

1 TSP. BAKING SODA

1 C. SUGAR

½ TSP. SALT

5 TBSP. VEGETABLE OIL

1 TBSP. APPLE CIDER VINEGAR (SEE NOTE #2)

1 TSP. VANILLA

1 C. COLD WATER

PREHEAT OVEN TO 350. Dump all of the ingredients into a square (8 x 8 or 9 x 9) pan. Mix well with a fork. Bake for 30 minutes. Cool completely. Great with a glass of milk!

Note #1: Since you aren't using beaters to smooth out the batter, you can sift the flour before adding it for a slightly smoother texture. But let's face it—this is a great cake even if you don't sift the flour, and sifting sort of defeats the purpose if you're going for a fast, easy recipe. If you don't sift, just mix well with the fork.

Note #2: The vinegar is critical for the cake to rise properly. Don't leave it out! You can substitute white vinegar if you don't have apple cider vinegar.

Unexpected Post Script:

I literally dusted this recipe off and made it for the first time in my children's lives while testing recipes for this book. I'll never know why I waited so long—it was a cake I loved as a child, after all. After tasting it, two daughters immediately demanded they have two-layered Cockeyed Cakes for their birthdays. Since this cake isn't meant to be taken out of the pan, but eaten one piece at a time (and therefore the whole thing doesn't slide right out into a nice, pretty layer), I had to improvise.

I lined the cake pans with well-buttered parchment so I could get each of the two cakes out of the pans. But with the parchment in the pan, I had to mix the batter in a bowl instead of in the pan, sort of defeating the "cockeyed" ease of the recipe.

I frosted the whole double-layered cake with Classic Chocolate Buttercream Icing (see p. 170). The final result was great, and both daughters were very pleased, even though this cake was never in a million years meant to be used that way.

A few years ago, Mars, Inc. stopped marketing the Mars Bar candy bar—but they didn't stop making it. In its place, the company now sells the exact same bar with a new name: Snickers Almond. Did you realize it's the exact same candy bar? In Europe and elsewhere, the same candy bar is sold as Mars Almond. Confused yet? Let's make it worse. A candy bar marketed to Europeans and others outside the United States as the Mars Bar is called the Milky Way in the United States.
Wait. What?
Even more confused? It gets worse.
Buy a "Milky Way" while vacationing abroad, and you'll get what you know here as a "3 Musketeers" bar.

Money talks, but chocolate sings.

I have to admit having fun with this one. By the time I reached it in my experiments, I'd done enough in my chocolate "laboratory" to avoid "destroying" recipes (my daughter's words). This is my personal twist on a classic.

Classic Chocolate Sheet Cake

½ C. SOUR CREAM

1 TSP. BAKING SODA

2 STICKS BUTTER, MELTED AND SLIGHTLY COOLED

1 C. MILK

2 EGGS

1 TSP. VANILLA

¼ C. COCOA

½ TSP. SALT

2 C. SUGAR

2 C. FLOUR

PREHEAT OVEN TO 350. Grease a standard-size jelly-roll pan with nonstick spray. In a small bowl, mix the sour cream and baking soda. Set aside; the mixture will puff up. In a separate mixing bowl, combine the cooled melted butter, milk, eggs, and vanilla; beat until well blended. Once the sour cream mixture has puffed up, add it and mix well. Add the cocoa, salt, sugar, and flour, scraping the sides of the bowl as needed. Pour the batter into the prepared pan and spread evenly. Bake for about 25 minutes, or until a tooth-pick inserted near the center comes out clean. Immediately after removing the cake from the oven, frost with your favorite frosting. Alternate: If you don't want to use frosting, sprinkle 1–2 C. choco-late chips across the top of the hot cake; wait 5 minutes for the chips to melt, then spread gently with a rubber scraper for a thin "icing" of pure chocolate heaven. Cut the cake into pieces just be-fore the chocolate is totally hard so the "icing" doesn't crack.

Mom is both a chocoholic and a health nut. That means she believes the closer you get to the source of the original food, the better, because that's the way nature made it. (Did you know that the closer you get to natural chocolate, the healthier it is? Pure chocolate, without added sugars and fats, is one of the healthiest foods on the planet!) Mom has invented "real-food" chocolate recipes, and her famous chocolate cake is one of them. It's particularly good with Mom's Honey Chocolate-Mousse Icing (p. 176).

Mom's Real-Food Chocolate Cake

2 C. WHOLE-WHEAT FLOUR

2 C. WHOLE SUGAR (BROWN SUGAR, SUCANAT, RAPADURA, ETC.)

½ C. COCOA

½ C. APPLESAUCE

½ C. COCONUT OIL

1 C. WATER

1 TBSP. APPLE CIDER VINEGAR

1 TBSP. VANILLA EXTRACT

WATER

2 EGGS

1½ TSP. BAKING SODA

PREHEAT OVEN TO 350. Grease a 9 x 13 baking pan (or use nonstick cooking spray). In a large bowl, combine flour, sugar, and cocoa. In a small saucepan, combine applesauce, coconut oil, and 1 C. water. Bring to a boil, stirring constantly. Pour the hot oil mixture into the dry ingredients and blend on low speed or by hand. In a measuring cup, combine the apple cider vinegar and vanilla extract; add enough water to make ½ C. liquid. Pour the liquid into the batter and blend. Add the eggs and blend again. Finally, mix in the baking soda. The batter will be runny. Pour into the greased baking pan and bake for 30–35 minutes, or until a toothpick inserted near the center comes out clean. Cool and frost.

Note: "Real-food" does not mean low-fat. It also does not mean low-calorie. And it doesn't mean poor flavor, which a lot of people assume. What it *does* mean is that you're using real ingredients that you might not otherwise think about, like unprocessed sugar and whole-wheat flour—and perhaps a few other ingredients you might not normally associate with chocolate cake.

It took eight batches before I got this one, as Goldilocks would say, "just right." Part of the reason for that is because it's one of the very first recipes I began playing with, back before I knew much about the chemistry of baking, how temperamental chocolate can be, and how to handle chocolate properly. The seventh version was pretty darn good, but I had a great idea for making it even better, so I couldn't resist. Close to the end of the recipe-testing process, I tried one more batch. I'm so glad I did!

Sinful Chocolate Cupcakes

½ C. BUTTER

2 TSP. BAKING SODA

1 C. SOUR CREAM

2 EGGS

1 TSP. VANILLA

1 C. SUGAR

1 TSP. BAKING POWDER

2 C. FLOUR

¼ C. COCOA

PREHEAT THE OVEN TO 400. Put paper baking cups into a cupcake pan. In a small bowl, melt the butter in the microwave; cool in the freezer for about 5 minutes. Meanwhile, in a small bowl, combine the baking soda and sour cream. Stir well and set aside. The mixture will puff up as it sits. In a large bowl, beat the eggs and vanilla. Add the cooled butter and puffed-up sour cream mixture. Add the sugar and mix well. Add the baking powder, flour, and cocoa; beat for a minute or two until the batter is fully mixed. Spoon the batter into the cupcake liners and bake for about 18 minutes. Cool and ice with your favorite icing. Makes 1 dozen.

There's nothing better than a good friend, except a good friend with chocolate.

Imagine a cake where each bite brings one of three slightly different kinds of chocolate bliss to your mouth. Then try this recipe, because that's precisely what it offers.

Chocolate Baked Alaska

CAKE (SEE DIRECTIONS)

HALF A GALLON OF ICE CREAM (SEE DIRECTIONS)

MAKING THE MERINGUE & PUTTING IT ALL TOGETHER:

⅔ C. SUGAR

3 TBSP. COCOA

3 EGG WHITES

½ TSP. CREAM OF TARTAR

HALF A GALLON OF ICE CREAM

YOU'LL NEED:

One layer of a chocolate cake, covered in plastic wrap and frozen for 2 hours, then cut in half. It can be one layer of the Two-Layer Chocolate Birthday Cake (p. 24)—I'm sure you'll come up with something to do with the other layer—Devil's Food Cake (p. 14), or even Cockeyed Cake (p. 16). If using Cockeyed Cake, follow the note below that recipe so you can get it out of the pan. The cake you choose doesn't really matter. Just wrap it up in plastic so it doesn't get freezer burn, wait until it gets hard, and then cut it in half.

HALF A GALLON OF ICE CREAM

Use whatever flavor you want. Store-bought ice cream is fine, of course, but if you happen to have something homemade on hand, be prepared for chocolate heaven. Take the ice cream out of the freezer about half an hour before you use it so it can soften

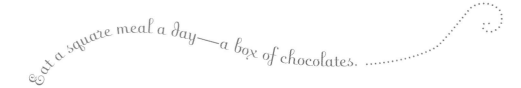

Eat a square meal a day—a box of chocolates.

enough to dig into and spread a bit. You don't want it liquid—just soft enough to work with.

PREHEAT THE OVEN TO 450. Cover a cookie sheet with parchment. Put the bottom half of the cake on the cookie sheet; set the top half aside. Spread the ice cream on the lower half of the cake; put the top half over the ice cream. Sift the sugar and cocoa; set aside. In a separate bowl on high speed, beat the egg whites and cream of tartar until thick and foamy. Gradually beat in the sugar and cocoa mixture, about 2 Tbsp. at a time, until incorporated and the whites are stiff and glossy. Spread the meringue over the cake, making sure to seal the cake completely, including where the cake touches the pan. The heat should reach only the meringue. Bake for only 5–6 minutes, just until the meringue starts to brown. Serve immediately. Note: You can refreeze the cake and serve it later frozen, but that's not nearly as fun as serving hot meringue with cold ice cream inside!

Who cares if it melts in your hand?

This is another easy recipe that (eventually) turned out really great. My twelve-year-old helped with the various versions, offering her own suggestions, and we both celebrated the final result. We filled the layers with a vanilla pudding/whipping cream combination and covered the whole thing with a Ganache Icing glaze (p. 171), but you can do whatever yummy chocolate thing you want with it.

Two-Layer Chocolate Birthday Cake

2 EGGS

⅔ C. HOT COCOA MADE AT THE STRENGTH OF 1 C., HOT

2 OZ. BAKING CHOCOLATE, ROUGHLY CHOPPED

⅔ C. OIL

⅔ C. SOUR CREAM

1 TSP. VANILLA

1⅓ C. SUGAR

1 C. FLOUR

⅔ C. COCOA

1 TSP. BAKING SODA

½ TSP. BAKING POWDER

PREHEAT OVEN TO 325. Grease two 8-inch round pans well. Place a piece of parchment in the bottom of each pan; grease the parchment. In a large bowl, beat the eggs until they're light and fluffy, at least 5 minutes. (An electric hand mixer works great but can be tiring. If using a stand-alone mixer, use the whisk attachment for this part and then switch to the paddle for the rest of the recipe.) In the meantime, make the hot cocoa. While it's still hot, add the chopped chocolate to the hot cocoa; whisk until the chocolate is melted and combined thoroughly. Gradually add the oil, sour cream, vanilla, and cocoa/chocolate mixture to the eggs. Scrape the sides as needed, then beat for 2 minutes. In a separate bowl, combine the sugar, flour, ⅔ C. cocoa, baking soda, and baking powder. Gradually add the dry ingredients to the batter and mix well. Divide the batter

All happiness depends on a chocolate breakfast.

equally between the two round pans and bake for about 50 minutes, or until a toothpick inserted into the center comes out clean. Remove from pans. Peel off the parchment and turn right-side up. Cool, layer, and ice as desired.

A good piece of chocolate has about 200 calories. I enjoy two servings per night, and a few more on weekends, so I consume 3,500 calories of chocolate each week—which equals one pound of weight per week.
Therefore . . .
In the last three and a half years,
I have eaten the equivalent of about 180 pounds in chocolate.
I weigh 165 pounds. Without chocolate,
I would have wasted away to nothing
about three months ago!
I owe my life to chocolate.
—DeLayna B.

Ice Cream-Filled Chocolate Cake Rolls

1 C. FLOUR

1½ TSP. BAKING POW-DER

2 TBSP. COCOA

3 EGGS

1 C. SUGAR

½ C. WATER

1 TSP. VANILLA

PREHEAT OVEN TO 375. Grease a jelly-roll pan, line it with parchment, and grease the parchment. In a small bowl, blend the flour, baking powder, and cocoa. In a separate bowl, beat the eggs until they're thick and lemon-colored (if you're using a stand-alone mixer, use the whisk attachment; a paddle attachment doesn't have the power to do the job). This may take as long as 10 minutes. Keep going until the eggs are thick; they're the basis for the rest of the cake. Gradually beat in the sugar. On low speed, add the water and vanilla. Mix in the dry ingredients (switch to the paddle attachment at this point). Mix just until the batter is smooth. Pour into the pan, smooth out evenly, and bake for 12–15 minutes. Immediately cut around the edges with a butter knife. Turn upside down on a dish towel that's slightly larger than your cake. Sprinkle a second dish towel of the same size with cocoa powder (use a small sieve with cocoa in it and tap the sieve with a spoon to sprinkle the cocoa). Quickly put the sprinkled towel over the cake. Flip the cake so the

Got chocolate?

"pretty" side is down, facing the cocoa-sprinkled towel; that will be the outside of the cake. (If you can, use two people to flip so you can hold all four corners of the towels.) If needed, cut any crusty edges off the cake, and carefully roll it into a spiral, starting from the narrow end. Set it aside to cool. When the cake has completely cooled, unroll it very carefully and spread the interior with about half an inch of your choice of filling. (Don't overfill, or it'll ooze out.) If you're using ice cream, take the container out of the freezer about half an hour beforehand to let it soften enough to spread. Re-roll the cake. If using ice cream, wrap the roll in plastic wrap to prevent freezer burn. Refreeze the roll for about an hour. Take out of the freezer a few minutes before serving so it can soften enough to slice with a knife; run the knife under warm water before slicing.

Great ice creams to use for filling:
Classic Chocolate (p. 88)
Mint Chocolate Chip (p. 83)
Vanilla
Cookies and Cream (p. 89)
Strawberry
Rocky Road
Chocolate Cherry Cordial (p. 90)

Other fillings:
White Chocolate Filling (p. 81)
Chocolate-Peanut Butter Filling (p. 179)
Classic Chocolate Mousse (p. 84)
Easy Chocolate Pudding (p. 87)

This recipe comes from fellow chocolate-lover, dear friend, and fellow writer, Josi Kilpack. I am not a great cook and do not love spending time in the kitchen, but Josi is and does, so I completely trusted her when she sent me this recipe. It turned out great on the first try. Best of all, not only is it delicious—it's quick and easy.

Hot Fudge Cake

2 C. FLOUR

3 C. SUGAR, DIVIDED

4 TSP. BAKING POWDER

½ TSP. SALT

1 C. COCOA, DIVIDED

1 C. BUTTER, MELTED
(COOL A LITTLE; IT
SHOULD NOT BE HOT)

1 C. MILK

2 TSP. VANILLA

1 C. NUTS, CHOPPED
(OPTIONAL)

3 C. HOT WATER

PREHEAT OVEN TO 350. In a 9 x 13 pan, combine flour, 1½ C. sugar, baking powder, salt, and ½ C. cocoa. Mix well. Add the butter and mix again. Add milk and vanilla, mixing with a fork until well blended. Use some muscle to get out the lumps as best you can. In a small bowl, combine the remaining 1½ C. sugar, remaining ½ C. cocoa, and nuts (if desired). Sprinkle this mixture over the batter in the pan. Pour 3 C. hot water over the entire pan. Do not stir. Bake for 40 minutes. Remove from oven; allow the cake to set for 10 minutes (it will finish baking outside the oven). The cake forms a cakelike crust on top with a puddinglike fudge layer underneath. Serve hot with vanilla ice cream on the side.

Life's short. Eat dessert first.

When searching out ideas for a chocolate cheesecake, I had to shake my head. There's apparently a huge misconception that chocolate desserts don't have to have much chocolate in them. One recipe had all of 3 ounces for a 9 x 13 pan. That's less than a handful of chocolate chips—for a huge pan. What are these people thinking? Surely they aren't chocoholics. When developing this cheesecake, I boosted the amount of chocolate to a respectable level, actually increasing it by several times. I mean, come on. If we're going to do chocolate, let's do it right, for Pete's sake.

Marbled Chocolate Cheesecake

CRUST:
1 CHOCOLATE-COOKIE CRUMB CRUST (P. 104)

FILLING:
16 OZ. (2 8-OZ. PKGS.) CREAM CHEESE, SOFTENED

½ C. SUGAR

1 TSP. VANILLA

½ C. SOUR CREAM

2 EGGS

1 C. SEMISWEET CHOCOLATE CHIPS, MELTED

TO PREPARE THE CRUST, follow directions for the Chocolate-Cookie Crumb Crust recipe, except put foil into an 11 x 7 glass dish, leaving several inches of foil hanging over the edges so you can later lift the entire cheesecake out of the dish before serving. Smooth the crust with your fingers to fill the bottom of the dish, but don't press it up the sides. Bake according to directions (about 12 minutes). Remove the crust from the oven and reduce the heat to 325. Cool the crust in the fridge. To make the filling, beat the softened cream cheese, sugar, and vanilla until smooth and creamy. Add the sour cream and mix well. Add the eggs, one at a time, mixing thoroughly between each one. Scrape the edges of the bowl as needed. Remove ¾–1 C. of the mixture into a small bowl and set aside. Add the melted chocolate chips to the rest of the mixture and combine well, scraping the sides as needed. When the crust is cool, pour the chocolate mixture into the crust and spread out evenly. Drop the rest of the cream cheese mixture over the top by

I never met a chocolate I didn't like.

small spoonfuls (there should be 8–10 spoonfuls). Being careful not to cut the crust, gently draw a butter knife through the layers in S shapes—back and forth horizontally as well as vertically—to create a marbled effect. Bake at 325 for about 40 minutes, or until the cheesecake is mostly set. Cool on a wire rack. Chill for several hours or even overnight before serving to help blend the flavors. This is a deliciously smooth cheesecake that looks impressive but is easy to make—just keep that part a secret.

I eat chocolate only on days that end with "Y."....

After being admitted at eighteen weeks of pregnancy and spending more than a hundred days in the hospital, Lynn broke the record for the longest stay at that hospital's neonatal unit in hopes of saving the life of her unborn baby. Her daughter was finally born, nine weeks early—young but alive and with a good prognosis, weighing in at 3 lbs. 2 oz. Exhausted, Lynn returned home, craving a giant bag of peanut M&Ms. She ate the whole thing in a day . . . then picked up the empty bag and realized with horror that it had contained . . . 3 lbs. 2 oz.—the exact weight of her baby.

Oh, yes, it is—a chocolate angel food cake. Nothing more needs to be said. After cooling, ice it with Devilish Vanilla Icing (p. 178). Then slice it, eat it, and try not to collapse from sheer joy. I dare you.

Crooked Halo Angel Food Cake

1 C. FLOUR (CAKE FLOUR IS IDEAL, BUT REGULAR FLOUR WORKS FINE)

1 C. POWDERED SUGAR

¾ C. COCOA

12 EGG WHITES

1½ TSP. CREAM OF TARTAR

1 C. SUGAR

¼ TSP. SALT

1½ TSP. VANILLA

½ TSP. ALMOND EX-TRACT

PREHEAT OVEN TO 375 (if using a nonstick angel food cake tube pan, reduce the temperature to 365). Sift the flour, powdered sugar, and cocoa; set aside. (Sifting is essential in this recipe!) In a large bowl and on medium speed, beat the egg whites and cream of tartar until foamy. Increase the speed to high. Gradually beat in the sugar, 2 Tbsp. at a time. With the last batch of sugar, add the salt, vanilla, and almond extract. Continue beating until the whites are stiff and glossy. Sprinkle the dry ingredients over the top of the egg mixture, ½ C. at a time, and use a rubber spatula to gently fold until the dry ingredients are integrated and disappear. Continue, ½ C. at a time, until all the dry ingredients are mixed in. Scoop the batter into an ungreased angel cake tube pan. Gently "cut" through the batter with a rubber scraper to remove any hiding air bubbles. Bake 30–35 minutes or until golden brown. To cool, invert the tube of the pan over a funnel or thin, long-necked bottle; allow the cake to cool completely upside down. To remove from the pan, run a thin blade around the outside wall and around the middle tube. Pop out the cake from the outer pan. Run a thin blade between the flat base and the cake until it releases. Ice with Devilish Vanilla Icing (p. 178). *Icing Tip:* Put a small amount of icing (no more than 1 C.) in a separate bowl. Use that icing to apply a thin layer to seal in the crumbs. (The separate bowl prevents any crumbs from getting into your main batch.) When you've sealed off the crumbs, apply a nice, thick layer of icing to the cake. For an extra "wow" factor when serving the cake, top with grated chocolate or chocolate curls (use a vegetable peeler pulled along a solid piece of chocolate).

Chocolate is an essential nutrient.

First created in the 1920s by the Girl Scouts, s'mores have become such a part of American life that even when we're not by a campfire toasting marshmallows, we want to experience the melded flavors of graham crackers, marshmallows, and chocolate. This has yielded a huge number of recipes for noncampfire versions, including baking them in the oven, microwaving them, or simply using the basic flavors in other foods, like a S'Mores pie.
National S'Mores Day is August 10. Be sure to celebrate!

This cake is also known as "The Most Dangerous Cake in the World" because you can get your chocolate fix within minutes—anytime, day or night. It's a huge single serving or two rather generous servings. This recipe has been floating around the Internet for so long that I have no idea who originally came up with it, but I figured no chocolate cookbook could be complete without it. And because I'm a tweaker, I added my own changes, because that's what I do.

3-Minute Microwave Chocolate Cake

¼ C. FLOUR

¼ C. SUGAR

2 TBSP. COCOA

1 EGG

3 TBSP. MILK

3 TBSP. OIL

A SPLASH OF VANILLA, MINT, OR ALMOND EXTRACT

3 TBSP. CHOCOLATE CHIPS (OPTIONAL, BUT WHO ARE WE KID-DING?)

PREHEAT OVEN TO 350. In a 12-oz. or larger mug, combine flour, sugar, and cocoa. Add the egg and mix thoroughly. Stir in the milk, oil, and extract, and mix until smooth. Add the chocolate chips if you're using them. (Ha ha! Of course you are.) Cook in the microwave for 3 minutes on high (1000 watts). The cake rises as it cooks—don't worry if it comes close to the top of the cup, because it settles slightly after cooking. When it has settled, tip it onto a plate. If it doesn't tip out immediately, the chocolate chips may have sunk to the bottom and stuck there; use a butter knife to loosen the cake and try again. Let the cake cool slightly before eating. This recipe is great with ice cream and even better digging in with a fork—and a friend.

Will work for chocolate.

This one is all about presentation. Oh, and encasing your favorite cheesecake inside a box made of a tasty, dense chocolate cake. Either way you look at it, it totally rocks.

Treasure Box Cheesecake

FILLING:

USE 1 BATCH OF YOUR FAVORITE CHEESECAKE RECIPE—TRY MARBLED CHOCOLATE CHEESE-CAKE (P. 30) OR ONE OF YOUR OWN.

THE TREASURE BOX:

5 EGGS

⅓ C. SUGAR

1 TSP. VANILLA

7 TBSP. FLOUR

¼ C. COCOA, SIFTED (FOR A STRONGER FLAVOR, USE SLIGHTLY MORE COCOA AND/OR USE A DARK COCOA)

4 TSP. BUTTER, MELTED

PREHEAT OVEN TO 400. Grease and line with parchment both an 8-inch square pan and an 11 x 7 pan. Let the parchment hang a few inches over each side of the 8-inch square pan like handles so you can easily lift out the cake later. Beat the eggs, sugar, and vanilla until fluffy. Add flour and cocoa. Mix well. Beat in the melted butter. Spoon slightly more than half of the batter into the square pan and the remainder of the batter into the rectangular pan. Spread each layer of batter so it covers the bottom. Bake for 15 minutes, just until firm. Let both cakes cool, then remove both from pans. Cut the crusty edges off the rectangular cake. Cut it lengthwise so you have two strips that are both 11 inches long. Stack the two pieces and cut them into 3-inch-tall slices that are just more than 1 inch wide. Cut the square cake into two very thin layers. Keeping the parchment (with the handles!) in the pan, place one layer back into the square pan with the cut side up. Using the slices from the

A day without chocolate is like . . . night.

rectangular pan, "wallpaper" the sides of the square pan, pressing the cake pieces down so they create a tight seam with the thin layer that's already in the pan. You now have the walls and bottom of your box. Spoon the cheesecake filling of your choice into the box, making sure it doesn't fill the box higher than the "walls." Top with the remaining layer of cake, completing the box. Chill until the cheesecake is firm. When ready to serve, remove the cake with the parchment handles and gently scoot it onto a serving dish. Dust with powdered sugar and/or cocoa or add other embellishments, like chocolate curls, Chocolate Glaze (p. 182), and whipping cream.

Chocolate: Here today . . . gone today.

The year: 1893.
The Location: The World's Columbian Exposition in Chicago.
Milton Hershey attends and is impressed by a European chocolate display. Currently a millionaire caramel maker,
Hershey soon buys up all the chocolate equipment and ships it back to his plant in Pennsylvania.
Fortunately for the rest of us, he declares caramels a fad, sells his business, and devotes the rest of his life to chocolate.

Cookies

This recipe was given to me by Josi Kilpack, one of my best friends, a chocoholic—oh, and a fellow writer and Whitney Award winner. As you can expect, it's awesome. Caramel and chocolate? How can you go wrong there?

Chocolate Rolo Cookies

1 C. SUGAR

1 C. BROWN SUGAR

2 STICKS BUTTER

2 EGGS

2 TSP. VANILLA

3 C. FLOUR (SEE NOTE)

¾ C. COCOA

1 TSP. BAKING SODA

40–50 ROLO CANDIES, UNWRAPPED (ONE STANDARD BAG OF ROLOS)

PREHEAT OVEN TO 375. Grease cookie sheets. Cream sugar, brown sugar, and butter. Add eggs and vanilla and mix well. Add flour (see Note below), cocoa, and baking soda. Mix until well combined. Add a little more flour if the dough is too sticky to work with your hands. Pinch off walnut-sized balls of dough and wrap a piece of dough around each Rolo. Place on cookie sheets a couple of inches apart. Bake 7–9 minutes, until the cookie is set but the top is still soft to the touch. Don't overcook, or the caramel will get hard. Let the cookies cool on the cookie sheet for about five minutes before transferring them to the wire racks; doing that will allow the cookie bottoms to set up and will prevent caramel from oozing out. Note: Josi uses 2½ C. flour. Maybe because of humidity, that little flour resulted in such sticky dough that it was totally unworkable for me. I had to add another ½ C. Use as much flour as you need to result in a workable dough.

This recipe is one of my mother's that I tweaked just a bit. Her version was very healthy; mine is mostly healthy. Both taste great. (I love anything with chocolate, orange flavoring, and pecans.) When I read over her ingredients list and saw a cup and a half of chocolate chips, I grinned. That's Mom! So many people skimp on the chocolate, but Mom never will.

Orange Pecan Whole-Wheat Chocolate Chip Cookies

1 C. WHOLE-WHEAT FLOUR

1 C. WHITE FLOUR

1 TBSP. BAKING POWDER

½ TSP. SALT

2 STICKS BUTTER

1 C. BROWN SUGAR

2 TSP. ORANGE EXTRACT

1 TBSP. VANILLA EXTRACT

2 EGGS

1 C. PECANS, CHOPPED

1½ C. CHOCOLATE CHIPS

PREHEAT OVEN TO 375. Grease cookie sheets. Blend flours, baking powder, and salt in a small bowl; set aside. In a separate bowl, cream butter and brown sugar. Add orange extract, vanilla extract, and eggs, one at a time, mixing well between each one. Mix well. Add flour mixture and mix until well combined. Stir in pecans and chocolate chips. Drop by rounded spoonfuls onto cookie sheet. Flatten slightly. Bake 9–12 minutes, until barely golden brown. Do not overbake; err on the side of underdone so they'll stay soft. Store in an airtight container or zip-style bag.

Man cannot live by chocolate alone, but woman can.

Candy doesn't have to have a point. That's why it's candy.
—Charlie in the 2005 film
Charlie and the Chocolate Factory

Chocolate Shortbread Cookies

1½ STICKS CHILLED BUTTER, CUT INTO SMALL CUBES

2 TSP. VANILLA

1 C. POWDERED SUGAR

4 EGG YOLKS

⅛ TSP. BAKING POWDER

⅛ TSP. SALT

½ C. COCOA

1⅔ C. FLOUR

PREHEAT OVEN TO 400. Coat 2 cookies sheets with nonstick spray. Combine butter, vanilla, powdered sugar, and egg yolks; beat on low speed until well combined. In a separate bowl, combine baking powder, salt, cocoa, and flour; mix with a wooden spoon. Add to the butter mixture all at once. Beat on low just until combined—no more than a minute, or else the dough may become tough. Using either a rounded tablespoon measure or a small ice-cream scoop, drop the cookies onto the sheets; each should be roughly the same size, approximately a domed tablespoon. Flatten each dome slightly with the palm of your hand. Bake just until done, about 10 minutes. Remove from the cookie sheet immediately and cool on a wire rack. Makes 1½–2 dozen.

Chocolate Oatmeal Haystacks

2 C. SUGAR

1 STICK BUTTER

½ C. MILK

2 TBSP. COCOA

1 TSP. VANILLA

½ C. CREAMY PEANUT BUTTER

3 C. OATMEAL

IN A HEAVY-BOTTOMED PAN, combine sugar, butter, milk, vanilla, and cocoa. Stir well and bring to a boil; boil for 2 minutes. Remove from heat; add the peanut butter and oatmeal. Drop by large spoonfuls onto parchment-covered cookie sheets. To set the cookies faster, put them in the fridge for at least an hour. Makes 15–18 3-inch cookies.

Families are like chocolate . . . mostly sweet, sometimes with a few nuts!

This recipe uses one of my favorite spices of all time: cardamom, something I fell in love with thanks to my Finnish heritage. Cardamom is a bit pricey in the U.S. and not nearly as fresh or strong-flavored as the Finnish stuff, but the smell alone makes my eyes roll with pleasure. If you're gun-shy of cardamom, replace it with ¼ tsp. nutmeg and ⅛ tsp. ground cloves. The cookies will still be great. When I first made these, I asked my two oldest kids for their reactions. My son thought there was too much chocolate, my chocoholic daughter said there was not enough. Since I wasn't sure how to take either suggestion, I left the recipe as it was.

Sierra Nuggets

2 STICKS BUTTER

1 C. BROWN SUGAR

1½ C. SUGAR

1 TBSP. MILK

1½ TSP. VANILLA

2 EGGS

1 C. CRUMBLED CORN-FLAKES (ABOUT 2 C. BEFORE CRUMBLING)

3 C. OATS

1¾ C. FLOUR

1¼ TSP. BAKING SODA

1 TSP. SALT

1½ TSP. CINNAMON

1–2 TSP. CARDAMOM (TO TASTE)

1 12-OZ. PKG. SEMI-SWEET CHOCOLATE CHIPS

1 C. WALNUTS, CHOPPED (OPTIONAL)

PREHEAT THE OVEN TO 375. Cream butter, brown sugar, and sugar. Add milk, vanilla, and eggs. Add cornflakes and oats. Mix well. In a separate small bowl, mix flour, soda, salt, cinnamon, and cardamom. Add to the batter and mix well. Mix in the chocolate chips and walnuts, if desired. Drop by spoonfuls onto greased cookie sheets and bake for 10–13 minutes, until just golden on the edges. Makes about 3 dozen.

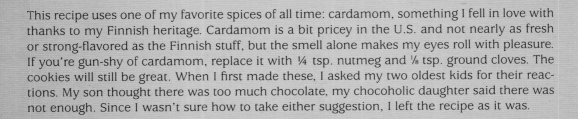

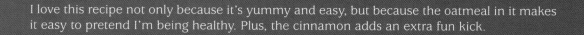

I love this recipe not only because it's yummy and easy, but because the oatmeal in it makes it easy to pretend I'm being healthy. Plus, the cinnamon adds an extra fun kick.

Double-Chocolate Oatmeal Cookies

1 STICK BUTTER

½ C. BROWN SUGAR

1 EGG

1 TSP. VANILLA

1¼ C. FLOUR

3 TBSP. COCOA

1 TSP. BAKING POWDER

½ TSP. BAKING SODA

½ TSP. SALT

1 TSP. CINNAMON

1¼ C. OATS

1 C. SEMISWEET CHOCOLATE CHIPS

PREHEAT TO 350. Cream the butter and brown sugar. Add the egg and vanilla. Add the flour, cocoa, baking powder, baking soda, salt, and cinnamon. Mix well. Add the oats until completely moistened. Stir in the chocolate chips. Drop onto a cookie sheet by spoonfuls and bake for 9–11 minutes. The cookies will still be very soft. Let them finish baking on the cookie sheet for an additional 10 minutes before letting them completely cool on wire racks. Makes about 1½ dozen.

The peanut butter chips here don't add a huge punch, so if you're not a huge fan of peanut butter, no worries—you'll probably still like these cookies. They add just a hint to what's already a wow chocolate cookie.

Peanut Butter and Chocolate Chip Cookies

1 C. SUGAR

¾ C. BROWN SUGAR

2 STICKS BUTTER

1 TSP. VANILLA

2 EGGS

1¾ C. FLOUR

1 C. OAT FLOUR (ABOUT 1⅓ C. OATS BEFORE BLENDING INTO FLOUR)

½ C. COCOA

1 TSP. BAKING SODA

¼ TSP. SALT

¾ C. PEANUT BUTTER CHIPS (I PREFER REESE'S BRAND—THEY TASTE BETTER THAN OTHERS)

½ C. SEMISWEET CHOCOLATE CHIPS

PREHEAT OVEN TO 350. Grease cookie sheets. With an electric mixer in a large bowl, beat sugar, brown sugar, butter, vanilla, and eggs. Mix in flour, oat flour, cocoa, baking soda, and salt until well blended. Add peanut butter chips and chocolate chips, mixing just until they're incorporated. Drop by heaping spoonfuls onto cookie sheets and bake for 10–12 minutes or just until cookies are set. Makes about 2 dozen.

And above all . . . think chocolate! —Betty Crocker

Jumbo Rocky Road Cookies

1⅓ C. SEMISWEET CHOCOLATE CHIPS, MELTED

¾ STICK (6 TBSP.) BUTTER

2 EGGS

¾ C. SUGAR

2 TSP. DARK CHOCOLATE HOT COCOA POWDER (OPTIONAL, BUT IT GIVES A KICK TO THE FLAVOR)

2 TSP. VANILLA

½ TSP. SALT

¼ TSP. BAKING POWDER

¼ C. FLOUR

Ingredients continued on next page.

PREHEAT OVEN TO 350. Line 3 cookie sheets with foil. (You don't need to grease the foil, but you must use foil; parchment or greased cookies sheets won't work.) In a medium, microwave-safe glass bowl, melt the 1⅓ C. chocolate chips and butter for 1 minute. Stir; heat again for another 30 seconds. Repeat until chocolate is barely melted (don't let it scorch). Set aside to cool slightly. In a separate mixing bowl on high speed, beat the eggs, sugar, cocoa powder, vanilla, salt, and baking powder for at least 2 minutes (it may take longer), until the mixture is a pale tan and starts to develop small bubbles. On low speed, mix in the chocolate/butter mixture. Add the flour; mix just until incorporated. Mix in the 1 C. chocolate chips and almonds. Using a ¼-cup measure, drop a cookie at the corners of each cookie sheet, leaving plenty of room for the cookies to spread. The dough should be nice and rounded on top—they'll flatten and spread out on their own, so

1 C. SEMISWEET CHOCOLATE CHIPS

1 C. ALMONDS, SLIVERED OR ROUGHLY CHOPPED

1–1½ C. MINIATURE MARSHMALLOWS

don't press them down. Bake 11–12 minutes. Remove from the oven just long enough to press marshmallows into the top of each cookie—each cookie can probably hold about 10. Return to the oven for an additional 2–3 minutes so the cookies can finish baking and the marshmallows can toast slightly (don't let them melt). Slide the foil with the baked cookies onto a cooling rack. When the cookies are fully cooled, peel them off the foil. Makes 1 dozen.

Chocolate story from Colleen:
When my youngest had his two-year exam, the pediatrician suggested seeing a speech therapist because my son was behind on his speech. I wasn't too worried, because his brother had been behind at that age and caught up, but I figured I'd better start working with him. I tried to get him to repeat words each time I suggested a food. His response was always, "No!" Then out of the blue, he offered a food he wanted, saying clearly and perfectly, "Chocolate!" I didn't even know he knew the word. Shocked, I repeated it. "You want chocolate?"
With a nod and a grin, he repeated it. "Chocolate."
What followed was a wonderful bonding moment over a little bowl of chocolate chips.

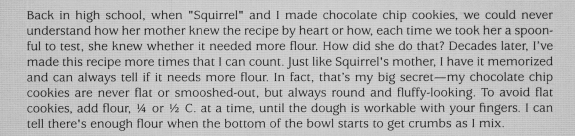

Back in high school, when "Squirrel" and I made chocolate chip cookies, we could never understand how her mother knew the recipe by heart or how, each time we took her a spoonful to test, she knew whether it needed more flour. How did she do that? Decades later, I've made this recipe more times that I can count. Just like Squirrel's mother, I have it memorized and can always tell if it needs more flour. In fact, that's my big secret—my chocolate chip cookies are never flat or smooshed-out, but always round and fluffy-looking. To avoid flat cookies, add flour, ¼ or ½ C. at a time, until the dough is workable with your fingers. I can tell there's enough flour when the bottom of the bowl starts to get crumbs as I mix.

Classic Chocolate Chip Cookies

2 STICKS BUTTER

¾ C. SUGAR

¾ C. BROWN SUGAR

2 EGGS

1 TSP. VANILLA

1 TSP. SALT

1 TSP. BAKING SODA

3 C. FLOUR (MORE OR LESS—THE EXACT AMOUNT WILL DEPEND ON THE HUMIDITY IN YOUR AREA, AMONG OTHER FACTORS)

1 C. (HALF A 12-OZ. BAG) SEMISWEET CHOCOLATE CHIPS

PREHEAT OVEN TO 375. Cream the butter, sugar, and brown sugar. Add the eggs and vanilla; mix well. Add the salt and soda. Gradually add the flour, starting with about 2 C., adding ¼ to ½ C. at a time until the dough is no longer sticky and crumbs begin to form at the bottom of the bowl. You should be able to pinch the dough without getting any on your fingers. Add the chocolate chips; mix just enough to incorporate them. Bake on greased cookie sheets for 9–11 minutes. Take them out just when they're starting to get golden edges. They won't look completely baked. Let the cookies cool on the sheets for about 10 minutes before removing and cooling completely on wire racks. Makes about 2½ dozen.

Note: Since this recipe uses butter instead of shortening or margarine, store the cookies in airtight containers so they stay soft longer. These cookies are great for baking in convection ovens—you can bake an entire batch (two or three trays) at once.

These are cookies with no flour but with plenty of taste. It didn't occur to me when I was first making them, but later on as I was recording my experiment, I smiled. My cousin and several members of her family have celiac disease, which prevents them from eating gluten—and that includes anything with flour. At one point, she half-jokingly requested that I have at least one recipe in my cookbook that she could make for her family. While there are recipes in these pages that have no gluten in them, this is definitely one kids will like. Jodee, this one's for you and your little guys.

Chocolate-Coconut Macaroons

BUTTER FOR GREASING BAKING SHEETS

½ C. SEMISWEET CHOCOLATE CHIPS

½ C. MILK CHOCOLATE CHIPS

4 EGG WHITES

1 TSP. CREAM OF TARTAR

1¼ C. SUGAR

1 TSP. ALMOND EXTRACT (OR VANILLA, AS PREFERRED)

3 C. SHREDDED COCONUT

PREHEAT OVEN TO 325. Use butter to grease three baking sheets (rub a hard stick of butter directly on the sheet, or use a brush to spread softened butter); nonstick spray doesn't provide enough grease to release these cookies. In a small bowl, melt the two kinds of chocolate chips; mix well. In a separate bowl that's free of any trace of grease or water, beat the egg whites until fluffy. Add the cream of tartar. When the whites have formed stiff peaks and while still beating, gradually pour in the sugar, about 2 Tbsp. at a time. Continue beating until the whites have softened slightly, another couple of minutes. Add the melted chocolate chips and the extract (almond or vanilla). Gently mix with a rubber scraper, folding until the mixture is brown throughout (no white should show through, even in little streaks). Stir in the coconut, mixing just until the coconut is fully integrated. Don't mix too much, or you'll lose the loft of the whites.

Using two soup spoons, drop tablespoonfuls of batter onto the buttered baking sheets. Bake for 9–11 minutes, until the tops are hardened to the touch and starting to brown. Cool on the sheet for a couple of minutes, and transfer to a wire rack to finish cooling. Makes 3–4 dozen.

Chocolate as Aspirin? Dark Chocolate, That Is
According to an article on FoodNavigator—USA.com, cocoa can act on platelets much the same way aspirin does—and thus prevent heart attacks. The irony? Some volunteers for the trial were disqualified because they were eating chocolate—apparently a no-no for the study. Even though they were kicked out, their blood was tested anyway and compared with that of others.
The results? "The chemical in cocoa beans has a biochemical effect similar to aspirin in reducing platelet clumping, which can be fatal if a clot forms and blocks a blood vessel, causing a heart attack. Eating a little bit of chocolate or having a drink of hot cocoa as part of a regular diet is probably good for personal health, so long as people don't eat too much of it, and too much of the kind with lots of butter and sugar."
So not only is chocolate good for you, but it's very good for you: The researchers say that a few squares of dark chocolate each day can reduce the risk of a heart attack by almost 50 percent in some people!
As if you needed an excuse.

Brownie Cookie Bites

2 C. SUGAR

3 ½ C. FLOUR

1 TSP. BAKING POWDER

1 TSP. SALT

½ C. COCOA

¾ C. WATER

1 EGG

½ C. POWDERED SUGAR

PREHEAT TO 350. Grease cookie sheets. In a large bowl, combine sugar, flour, baking powder, salt, and cocoa. Add water and egg; mix well with a wooden spoon. Place the powdered sugar in a small bowl. Drop cookie dough by spoonfuls and shape into balls; roll balls in powdered sugar until covered. Place balls on cookie sheet and bake for 12–15 minutes or until touching a cookie with your finger leaves only a very slight indentation. Cool on a wire rack. Note: To keep these cookies soft, store them in an airtight container after they've cooled completely. On the other hand, if you're like me and love chewy brownies, let them sit out overnight, and they'll take on that awesome chewy brownie texture.

Chocolate is proof that God loves us and wants us to be happy.

When I invented these, my oldest daughter said, "These are okay" (code for, "I love these!"). She promptly inhaled three cookies fresh from the oven—and would have downed more if I hadn't shooed her off to do homework. I took that as a sign that they turned out pretty tasty. My kids learned early in life that the silver bag of Guittard chocolate chips was for eating, not for baking. This recipe is so yummy it deserves those chips. It makes a large enough batch that true chocoholics could use a bag and a half or even two full bags of chips, but one will do the job just fine for most people.

Milk Chocolate Chip Hazelnut-Flavored Cookies

5 C. FLOUR (OR MORE IF DOUGH IS TOO STICKY)

¾ C. HAZELNUT-FLAVORED COFFEE CREAMER POWDER, SUCH AS COFFEE-MATE®

½ TSP. BAKING SODA

½ TSP. SALT

1 C. SUGAR

½ C. BROWN SUGAR

2 STICKS BUTTER

Ingredients continued on next page.

PREHEAT OVEN TO 350. Grease cookies sheets with nonstick spray. In a medium bowl, combine flour, hazelnut-flavored creamer powder, baking soda, and salt. Mix well and set aside. In a separate bowl, cream sugar, brown sugar, and butter; add eggs, vanilla, and sweetened condensed milk, beating at medium speed until light and fluffy. Gradually add the flour mixture. If the dough is still sticky to the touch after it is mixed, add more flour, ¼ C. at a time, until the dough doesn't stick to your fingers. Stir in chocolate chips last. Drop by large spoonfuls (about 1½ inches in diameter) onto cookie sheets, about two inches apart. Bake for 10–12 minutes, until

Home is where the chocolate is.

56

2 EGGS

2 TSP. VANILLA

1 CAN SWEETENED CONDENSED MILK

1 PKG. (2 C.) OR MORE MILK CHOCOLATE CHIPS (I PREFER GUITTARD)

edges start to get slightly golden. Let the cookies cool on the baking sheets for 2–3 minutes before transferring them onto cooling racks. Makes about 4 dozen cookies.

Who cares if it melts in your hand?

Chocolate confession from Theresa:
For some reason, when I am pregnant, I lose weight. With my last child, I lost 22 pounds. The only change in my diet? I gave up chocolate.
As soon as I had the baby and began eating chocolate again, I gained back all of that weight—and then some. After seeing this happen with all three of my children, you'd think I'd get a clue and give up chocolate to keep the weight off.
I can't! I'm addicted!

Brownies, Bars, & Other Single-Serving Bliss

If you're a Rocky Road ice cream fan (like I am), you'll love these bars. You can use whatever nuts you want: chopped walnuts, almonds, or (my favorite) pecans.

Rocky Road Bars

CHOCOLATE COOKIE BASE:

1 STICK BUTTER

½ C. SUGAR

½ C. BROWN SUGAR

1 TSP. VANILLA

1 EGG

1½ C. FLOUR

⅔ C. COCOA

½ TSP. BAKING SODA

TOPPING:

1 8-OZ. PKG. CREAM CHEESE, SOFTENED

½ C. SUGAR

Ingredients continued on next page.

Ingredients continued on next page.

PREHEAT OVEN TO 350. Spray a 9 x 13 pan with nonstick cooking spray; line with foil, then spray again—even better, grease the foil with butter. (DO NOT skip this step. If you don't use foil and grease the foil, the cookie layer will stick like glue to the pan, and you won't be able to cut the bars out). For the cookie base, cream the butter, sugar, and brown sugar. Add the vanilla and egg; mix well. Add the flour, cocoa, and baking soda; mix well. Dump the dough into the foil-lined baking pan and press into a smooth layer with your fingers, covering the entire pan. Make the topping by combining the cream cheese, sugar, butter, flour, vanilla, and egg with an electric mixer until smooth. Add nuts. Spread over the cookie dough base. Sprinkle the chocolate chips evenly over the topping. Bake for

I never met a carbohydrate I didn't like.

60

¼ C. (½ STICK) BUTTER

2 TBSP. FLOUR

1 TSP. VANILLA

1 EGG

¼ C. NUTS, CHOPPED

1 C. SEMISWEET
CHOCOLATE CHIPS

2 C. MINIATURE
MARSHMALLOWS

MOM'S NUTTY CHOCO-
LATE ICING (SEE P. 177)

26–29 minutes, until the topping is set. Remove from oven; sprinkle the miniature marshmallows over the top. Return to the oven for about 2 more minutes to toast the marshmallows. Remove and cool on a wire rack. When fully cooled, drizzle with Mom's Nutty Chocolate Icing.

Life should not be a journey to the grave with the intention of arriving safely in an attractive and well-preserved body, but rather to skid in sideways, chocolate raised high in both hands, body thoroughly used up, totally worn out, and screaming, "Woohoo! What a ride!"

This recipe is easy, if a bit messy. My kids have a ball shaping the "marbles" and covering them in the chocolate. When they help, it's a quick and easy project . . . with the exception of some clean-up. Since the mess is mostly on your hands, it's not a big deal. If you let kids help, they'll probably just lick themselves clean like kittens.

Chocolate-Covered
Peanut Butter Pecan Marbles

MARBLE CENTERS:

1 PACKAGE GRAHAM CRACKERS (ABOUT 9), CRUSHED

1¼ C. POWDERED SUGAR (POSSIBLY MORE; SEE DIRECTIONS)

½ C. CREAMY PEANUT BUTTER

½ C. PECANS, FINELY CHOPPED

1 STICK BUTTER, MELTED

CHOCOLATE:

¾ –1 12-OZ. PKG. SEMI-SWEET CHOCOLATE CHIPS

3 TBSP. VEGETABLE OIL

CRUSH THE GRAHAM CRACKERS as finely as you can (a blender or food processor usually works well; you can also put the graham crackers in a zip-style plastic bag and crush them with a rolling pin). You should have approximately 1¼ C. crumbs. Add the powdered sugar, peanut butter, pecans, and melted butter; mix well with a wooden spoon. The mixture should hold together but not be very moist. (If the balls fall apart in the chocolate, the mixture is too moist; add an extra tablespoon or so of powdered sugar, mix well, and try dripping again.) Set aside. In a medium bowl, melt the chocolate chips and vegetable oil, following guidelines in the "Melting Chocolate" section on pp. 5–7; using a rubber scraper, mix the melted chocolate and oil together until it's smooth. Keep stirring, letting the heat of the rest of the chocolate melt any un-

For my birthday and Christmas, I'll take anything in a size chocolate.

62

melted bits. Roll a 1-inch scoop of the peanut butter mixture into a tight ball between your palms. Using a soup spoon, roll it around in the melted chocolate until it is fully coated with chocolate. Remove with the spoon and set on a layer of parchment on a cookie sheet. When the sheet is full, put it in the fridge to let the chocolate harden. Makes about 2 dozen marbles, depending on size.

In August 2006, a worker at a chocolate plant in Wisconsin got a bit more than he bargained for. The facility he worked in manufactures chocolate ingredients. Chocolate became stuck in one of the hoppers, and, like a good employee, he immediately tried pushing it back down. Then he fell in.
The 110-degree goop held him so tightly it might as well have been glue. After his rescuers added cocoa butter to thin the mixture, he was finally able to get out—some two hours later!

Chocolate Toasted Stacks

4 8-INCH FLOUR TORTI-
LLAS

3–4 TBSP. BUTTER,
MELTED

2 TBSP. SUGAR

½ TBSP. COCOA

¼ TSP. CINNAMON

½ C. SEMISWEET CHOCO-
LATE CHIPS, MELTED

4 OZ. CREAM CHEESE,
SOFTENED

¼ C. SUGAR

1 TSP. ALMOND EX-
TRACT (OR VANILLA,
WHICHEVER YOU PRE-
FER)

WHIPPED CREAM AND
CHOCOLATE SYRUP
FOR GARNISH

PREHEAT OVEN TO 400. Line two cookie sheets with foil or parchment and put two tortillas on each one. Lightly brush each tortilla
with melted butter. To make the base, combine 2 Tbsp. sugar, cocoa, and cinnamon; sprinkle the mixture over the tortilla pieces. (Tip:
Dump the mixture into a small sieve and then tap it with a spoon
over the tortillas to dust them evenly.) Put each cookie sheet in the
oven one at a time, and toast the tortillas for 5–7 minutes, until the
sugar mixture and butter mix and combine but the tortillas are
still flexible. Don't over-bake; the tortillas should not become hard.
Using a pizza cutter, slice each tortilla into 6 even pieces. Remove
the foil or parchment from the cookie sheet and let the pieces cool
completely while you make the filling: Beat the melted chocolate
chips, softened cream cheese, ¼ C. sugar, and extract (almond or
vanilla) until well combined and fluffy. For each serving, use three
tortillas pieces with filling between them. Spread 1 Tbsp. filling on

the first piece and place it on a plate. Spread 1 Tbsp. filling on the second piece and put it on top of the first one. Place one toasted piece on top for the final layer. Garnish with a dollop of whipped cream and a fancy drizzle of chocolate syrup. For extra punch, add sliced strawberries, blueberries, grated chocolate, or nuts.

The Chocolate Flower
The so-called "chocolate flower," Berlandiera Lyrata, *starts out about the size of a quarter but doesn't stay that way. By the time they're full grown, they're a tad too big for a Valentine's Day bouquet. Even so, tell your honey to plant some in your yard, and each time you sit on your porch, you'll inhale the sweet aroma of chocolate. Also called the Chocolate Scented Daisy, these flowers are native to the Southwest and are often bright yellow. They're known for attracting insects (if that's something you want to do). And, interestingly, the stamens even taste like unsweetened cocoa!*

I've always thought that Lemon Squares were a pleasant dessert—you know, very nice, but nothing I'd ever crave. Get me into the kitchen with chocolate, however, and I go a bit nuts.

Lemon Squares with a chocolate crust? This is definitely a version I can get into. I'd likely even crave these!

Chocoholic Lemon Squares

CRUST:

1 STICK + 2 TBSP. BUTTER

½ C. POWDERED SUGAR

1 TSP. VANILLA

⅓ C. COCOA

1 TSP. SALT

1 C. FLOUR

FILLING:

¼ C. FLOUR

2 C. SUGAR

4 EGGS

⅓ C. LEMON JUICE

TO MAKE THE CRUST: Preheat oven to 350. Line an 11 x 7 glass dish with parchment, leaving 2 inches hanging off each end to use as "handles" for removing the bars when they're done. Spray the parchment with nonstick spray. Cream butter, powdered sugar, and vanilla. Add cocoa, salt, and flour. Mix just until combined; if you over-mix, the dough will be tough. Using your fingers, press the dough evenly into the bottom of the dish. Bake for 15–18 minutes, or until done. Cool. To make the filling: Beat all filling ingredients together well and pour over crust. Bake at 350 for 35–40 minutes. Cool. Remove the bars by using the parchment "handles." Top them with a sprinkle of powdered sugar, Choco-Breakfast Topping (p. 138), and/or a drizzle of Chocolate Glaze (p. 182) before cutting into squares.

Here's a simple hint for chocolate brownies and bars: Always cut them with a plastic knife. Metal knives tend to attract baked chocolate like a magnet and pull at the brownies, making ragged cuts. Plastic knives (even the simple disposable kind) make cleaner cuts, especially if the brownies are even just a little warm. I have a Piglet knife left over from when my kids were little. I keep it around for nothing more than the important job of cutting brownies cleanly.

Perfect Chocolate Brownies

2 STICKS BUTTER, MELTED

2 C. SUGAR

4 EGGS

1+ TSP. VANILLA OR MINT EXTRACT (DEPENDING ON THE HOT COCOA MIX YOU USE; SEE BELOW)

1½ C. FLOUR

1 TSP. BAKING POWDER

1 TSP. SALT

¾ C. COCOA OR ½ C. COCOA + ¼ C. HOT COCOA MIX POWDER IN YOUR FAVORITE FLAVOR (SUCH AS RASPBERRY, BELGIAN CHOCOLATE, MINT, OR AMARETTO)

PREHEAT OVEN TO 350. Combine melted butter and sugar; blend with an electric mixer until the sugar melts and the mixture is smooth. Add the eggs and extract (vanilla or mint). Add remaining ingredients and mix well. Bake for 35 minutes in an ungreased 9 x 13 glass dish. To make these even more delicious:
—Sprinkle ½ C. chocolate chips over the top before baking.
—Immediately after taking the brownies from the oven, sprinkle the top with chocolate chips, let the chips melt, and then spread across the top as icing.

I am a woman of many moods. And all of them require chocolate.

This is a variation of Perfect Chocolate Brownies, but with the added bliss of caramel, pecans, and milk chocolate. It takes a bit longer to make, but the wait is worth it. They're particularly good with a scoop of ice cream on the side.

Gooey Turtle Brownies

2 C. SUGAR

4 EGGS

1 TSP. VANILLA

2 STICKS BUTTER, MELTED

1½ C. FLOUR

1 TSP. BAKING POWDER

1 TSP. SALT

¾ C. COCOA

12 OZ. CARAMEL ICE CREAM SAUCE

¾ C. PECANS, CHOPPED

¾ C. MILK CHOCOLATE CHIPS

PREHEAT OVEN TO 325. Cream sugar, eggs, and vanilla; add the melted butter and mix well. Add flour, baking powder, salt, and cocoa; mix well. Pour half the mixture into a greased 9 x 13 glass baking dish. Bake for 20 minutes. Remove from the oven. Drizzle the caramel sauce on top, followed by half of the pecans and half of the milk chocolate chips. Pour the rest of the brownie batter on top, either in a smooth layer or in drops from a spoon. Top with the remaining pecans and chocolate chips. Bake for an additional 35–40 minutes.

69

I saw a version of this kind of bar once—but with a white crust. Seriously? Chocolate bars without a chocolate crust? Surely you jest, I thought. So I had to invent my own proper version. The crust isn't heavy on the chocolate, but it's got a proper touch of chocolate. Like it should. When I first invented these bars, my taste testers consisted of my critique group and two twelve-year-olds who kept coming back for more. By the end of the night, the pan was nearly empty. I figured that was a pretty good sign.

Heavenly Chocolate Bars

CRUST:

½ C. BROWN SUGAR

1 STICK BUTTER

1 C. FLOUR

2 TBSP. COCOA

TOPPING:

2 EGGS

1 C. BROWN SUGAR

1 TSP. VANILLA

1 TSP. BAKING POWDER

½ TSP. SALT

1 C. MILK CHOCOLATE CHIPS

Ingredients continued on next page.

PREHEAT OVEN TO 350. For the crust, cream brown sugar and butter. Add the flour and cocoa; mix well. Press by hand into a greased 9 x 13 baking dish until mixture is spread evenly and covers the bottom of the dish. Bake for 10 minutes. While the crust bakes, in a medium bowl, create the topping: Mix the eggs, brown sugar, and vanilla with a spoon. Stir in the flour, baking powder, and salt; mix well. Stir in both kinds of chips. Pour over the crust and bake for an additional 15–20 minutes or until golden brown. Cool completely on a wire rack or in the fridge. To make the drizzle: In a microwave-safe glass bowl, melt the semisweet chocolate chips; start with one minute, stir, then heat at 30-second intervals until smooth. Stir the melted chocolate with a wooden spoon for about a minute before using it to allow it to temper and to prevent it from blooming when it cools. Pour melted chocolate into a freezer bag, cut off a corner, and drizzle the entire cup of melted chocolate over the top

1 C. PEANUT BUTTER CHIPS (OR IF YOU REALLY WANT A CHOCOLATE HANGOVER, SEMISWEET CHIPS)

DRIZZLE:

1 C. SEMISWEET CHOCOLATE CHIPS

of the bars in a checkerboard pattern, a zigzag pattern, or whatever design you like. Allow the drizzle to harden before cutting into bars and serving. These tend to be delicious but a bit gooey; you'll probably need a fork, but I doubt you'll complain about that.

Elga called it a dessert when she gave me the little handwritten index card [with the recipe], but I know she must have been kidding, because, um, see, Elga, it doesn't have any chocolate in it.
—Luisa Perkins, writer, blogger, and personal friend

Eat chocolate for breakfast, then you will start your day off right...

This recipe makes an entire cookie sheet of bars. That is either a very good thing or a very dangerous thing. To make matters worse, they're delicious and easy. Good luck.

Three-Layer Chocolate-Peanut Butter Bars

LAYER 1—CHOCOLATE COOKIE:

1 STICK BUTTER

1 C. SUGAR

1 C. BROWN SUGAR

1½ C. CREAMY PEANUT BUTTER

1 EGG

2 TSP. VANILLA

¼ C. WATER

¼ TSP. SALT

2 TSP. BAKING SODA

¼ C. COCOA

Ingredients continued on next page.

PREHEAT OVEN TO 350. To make the cookie: In a medium mixing bowl, beat the butter, sugar, brown sugar, and peanut butter until light. Add the egg, vanilla, and water; beat again until fluffy. One at a time, in this order and stirring as you go, add salt, baking soda, cocoa, and flour. Add the flour gradually, and only as much as needed—the dough should be slightly dry in the bowl and have the texture of cookie dough when pinched between your fingers. Press dough evenly into an ungreased cookie sheet. Bake for 10–12 minutes, just until it starts to get golden brown. Remove and cool completely. When the cookie layer is completely cooled, spread the Chocolate-Peanut Butter Icing over the top. To make the chocolate topping, slowly melt the chocolate chips and butter in the microwave, preferably in a Pyrex-type glass bowl, stirring often. When

A balanced diet is a truffle in both hands.

72

1¼–2 C. FLOUR, AS NEEDED

LAYER 2—CHOCOLATE-PEANUT BUTTER ICING (P. 179)

LAYER 3—CHOCOLATE TOPPING:

2 C. SEMISWEET CHOCOLATE CHIPS

1 STICK BUTTER

completely smooth, spread the topping evenly over the frosting layer. Allow to set. Just before the chocolate has set completely, cut into bars—cutting them before the chocolate completely sets prevents the chocolate topping from cracking when cut.

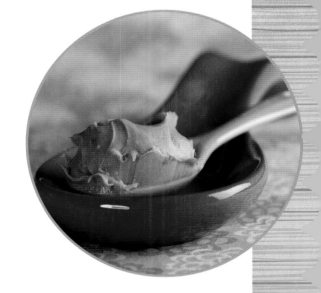

Inside some of us is a thin person struggling to get out, but she can usually be sedated with a few pieces of chocolate cake.
—Unknown

My kids couldn't get enough of these—and that includes my son, who's probably the least of the chocoholics in the family. "They're just so refreshing!" he kept saying. (Then I'd say, "Great! Now get off the carpet and eat it in the kitchen!") They're really fudgy (my favorite) and minty. Best of all, even though they're fattening, they're easy.

Peppermint Patty Fudge Brownies

3 STICKS BUTTER

3 C. SUGAR

1 TBSP. VANILLA

5 EGGS

2 C. FLOUR

1¼ C. COCOA

1 TSP. BAKING POWDER

1 TSP. SALT

1 12-OZ. PKG. PEPPERMINT PATTIES (ABOUT 24 PATTIES)

PREHEAT OVEN TO 350. Grease a 9 x 13 dish. In a large mixing bowl, cream the butter, sugar, and vanilla. Add the eggs and beat well. In a separate bowl, mix the remaining ingredients except the peppermint patties. Add to the wet ingredients and mix until well blended. Spread half the batter over the bottom of the pan. Layer the patties evenly over the mixture, being sure the edges of the patties touch each other but not the edges of the pan. Cover with the remaining half of the batter, covering the patties completely and sealing the edges. Bake for 45–50 minutes, just until the brownies start to pull away from the sides of the pan. Be careful not to overbake. Cool on a wire rack.

Broken candy bars don't have calories.

This is another great recipe from Mom's chocolate archive, one she no doubt invented herself. I love the way she thinks—she combines things no one else thinks of and then (of course) adds chocolate. These fill a standard jelly-roll pan, so they're perfect for a big crowd. Or lots of leftovers. Whichever.

Pumpkin and Meringue Chocolate-Chip Bars

BARS:

1 STICK BUTTER

1½ C. SUGAR

4 EGG YOLKS (RESERVE THE WHITES)

1 15-OZ. CAN PUMPKIN

½ TSP. SALT

½ TSP. BAKING SODA

2 TSP. BAKING POWDER

1 TSP. CINNAMON

¼ TSP. NUTMEG

2½ C. FLOUR

1 C. SEMISWEET CHOCOLATE CHIPS

Ingredients continued on next page.

PREHEAT OVEN TO 350. Coat a jelly-roll pan with nonstick spray. To make the bars: in a large mixing bowl, cream butter and sugar until light and fluffy. Blend in the egg yolks; add the pumpkin and mix well. Add the salt, soda, baking powder, cinnamon, and nutmeg. Add the flour and beat until all the dry ingredients are well incorporated. Add the chocolate chips and blend well. Spread evenly into the jelly-roll pan; bake for 10 minutes. (The bars will not be fully done at this point; they aren't supposed to be.) While the bars are baking, make the meringue topping: Whip the egg whites. When they are frothy, gradually add the sugar a tablespoon at a time, continuing to beat as you add the sugar. Beat until the whites have stiff peaks. After the bars have cooked for 10 minutes, remove them from the oven; sprinkle the top of the bars evenly with chocolate chips, covering the entire surface. Spread the meringue mixture evenly over the chocolate chips, sealing off the edges against the

MERINGUE TOPPING:

4 EGG WHITES (FROM SEPARATED YOLKS)

½ C. + 3 TBSP. SUGAR

1–2 C. SEMISWEET CHOCOLATE CHIPS

1 C. NUTS, CHOPPED (OPTIONAL)

pan. Sprinkle nuts (optional) over the top of the meringue. Bake another 20 minutes. Remove from the oven and cool before slicing and serving. Variation: Instead of making the meringue, add the nuts (if desired) to the bars and bake for a full 30 minutes until they are completely done. Let cool, then frost with Chocolate Cream Cheese Icing (p. 175).

Researchers recently discovered that one of the chemicals in chocolate, theobromine, is 30 percent more effective in reducing the activity on the vagus nerve than codeine. For those of us not in the medical field, the vagus nerve apparently is responsible for those nasty coughs, and codeine is often given to help quiet them down. If chocolate can soothe that nerve more effectively, researchers say, then it might behoove you to sit down with a cup of hot cocoa instead of a teaspoon of cough medicine!

Mousses, Pies, Puddings,
& Stuff in Bowls

This is basically a fancy way of saying, "Yowza, what a yummy chocolate pie." You can definitely use semisweet chocolate chips in this recipe, but if you do, the flavor will be very rich, and you'll probably be able to handle only one small piece at a time. Face it—that would be a tragedy. For the sake of those true chocoholics among us who want to eat lots of chocolate in a single sitting (I'm raising my hand), I suggest softening the flavor a tad by using milk chocolate chips.

Luscious Chocolate Tart

CRUST:

⅓ C. BUTTER

1 C. FLOUR

1 EGG, BEATEN

FILLING:

1 TBSP. BUTTER

1 14-OZ. CAN SWEET-ENED CONDENSED MILK

1 12-OZ. BAG MILK CHOCOLATE CHIPS

1 TSP. ALMOND EX-TRACT OR VANILLA EXTRACT

⅔ C. ALMONDS, CHOPPED

WHIPPED CREAM AND/OR CHOCOLATE FOR GARNISH

PREHEAT OVEN TO 400. For the crust: In a medium bowl, cut the butter and flour with a pastry blender (or use two butter knives, pulling them in opposite directions) until mixture is crumbly. Add the egg (make sure it's well beaten first, or it won't mix well into the crust). Stir until a dough forms. Press the dough firmly into a tart pan with a removable bottom or into a 9-inch pie tin. Bake for 12–14 minutes or until golden brown. Don't over bake. Cool on a wire rack. Reduce oven to 350. In a medium saucepan, create the filling: Melt butter over low heat. Add the sweetened condensed milk, chocolate chips, and almond or vanilla extract. Cook over low heat, stirring occasionally, until chocolate is melted. Stir in the almonds. Pour and spread evenly into the tart crust. Bake an additional 23–25 minutes or until the edges are set but the center still looks moist. Cool in the pan on a rack. Serve in slices, garnished with whipped cream and/or grated chocolate on top.

This recipe is virtually foolproof and oh-so-good inside chocolate cream puffs, between layers of a chocolate cake, inside éclairs, or anywhere else you need a filling. Including your tummy.

White Chocolate Filling

1 BOX OF INSTANT WHITE CHOCOLATE PUDDING MIX

1 C. WHIPPING CREAM

1 TBSP. POWDERED SUGAR

MAKE THE PUDDING according to package directions; refrigerate. While the pudding sets, whip the cream until firm and fluffy. Add the powdered sugar and mix it in on low. When the pudding is set, fold it into the whipped cream. Chill until ready to use. If using for cream puffs or éclairs, use the zip-bag trick (see p. 7) to fill them.

Countless numbers of people have eaten chocolate for breakfast and gone on to lead normal lives.

For chocoholics who think that the best possible combination is chocolate and peanut butter, this recipe is heaven in a pie crust. It's also simplicity in a pie crust. Use either a Chocolate-Cookie Crumb Crust (p. 104) or a purchased crust (chocolate or graham cracker both work great). I've even had this pie with a regular baked pie crust. With a filling this yummy, it's hard to consider that any crust would ruin it. The hardest part is waiting for it to set up, so plan ahead—make it early enough so that when you're ready, you can whip open the freezer door, top with a bit of whipped cream, and dig in.

Chocolate Peanut Butter Pie

2 OZ. UNSWEETENED BAKING CHOCOLATE

1 CAN SWEETENED CONDENSED MILK

½ C. CREAMY PEANUT BUTTER

1 C. WHIPPING CREAM

1 TSP. VANILLA

¼ C. POWDERED SUGAR

1 PREPARED PIE CRUST

IN A MICROWAVE-SAFE BOWL, melt the chocolate according to guidelines on pp. 5–7, stirring regularly at 30-second intervals. When the chocolate is melted, add the sweetened condensed milk and stir them well. Mix in the peanut butter. Allow the heat of the chocolate to melt the peanut butter and create a nice, smooth mixture. Set aside. In a separate bowl, whip the cream until light and fluffy (don't over beat, or you'll get butter); when whipped, add vanilla and powdered sugar. Mix in. Using a rubber scraper, fold the chocolate mixture into the whipping cream; scoop from the bottom of the bowl and lift to the top, turning the bowl and repeating until the two mixtures are fully combined and there are no more white spots. Pour the filling into the pie crust and put into the freezer for several hours (ideally, 6–8) until fully set. Top with whipped cream, grated chocolate, drizzled melted chocolate, or any other garnishes you'd like.

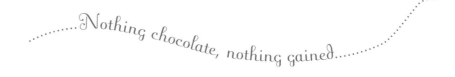

..........Nothing chocolate, nothing gained..........

Mint Chocolate Chip Ice Cream

6 C. HEAVY CREAM

3 C. MILK

2 C. SUGAR

1 TSP. SALT

2 TSP. MINT EXTRACT

10 DROPS GREEN FOOD COLORING (OPTIONAL; USE MORE OR LESS ACCORDING TO YOUR LIKING)

1–2 C. SEMISWEET CHOCOLATE, CHOPPED

IN A LARGE BOWL, combine cream, milk, sugar, salt, mint extract, and food coloring. Warm in the microwave for about 5 minutes to remove the chill and to help the sugar dissolve and integrate. (Alternately, you can combine the ingredients in a large pot and warm them on the stove for a few minutes. Don't get them hot or even very warm—you just want to remove the chill.) Stir until the sugar is completely dissolved. Stir in the chocolate. Pour the mixture into an ice cream maker container and freeze according to manufacturer's directions. You can serve the ice cream as soon as it freezes, but it tastes even better and gets less soft if you let it cure in the freezer for a few hours.

Notes:
You'll want small pieces of chopped chocolate, because huge chunks of frozen chocolate aren't pleasant to crack your teeth against. Use mini chocolate chips, chop up regular chocolate chips with a butcher knife, chop a chocolate bar, grate a solid chocolate bar, or even use a food processor to chop up a chocolate bar. (If you use a food processor, work quickly so you don't inadvertently melt the chocolate.) To lower the ice cream's fat content, you can reduce the cream and increase the milk to even amounts—4½ C. of each. The result will still taste great.

Chocolate mousse has a reputation for being really hard to make. And yes, there are those fancy-schmancy French chefs who do amazingly complex things with it. This recipe is close to the "fancy" ones, but it's still relatively simple. Important notes before you begin: When working with egg whites, use a copper or steel bowl. Both the bowl and beaters can have no trace of moisture or fat. Also, since egg whites gain more loft if they aren't cold, take them out of the fridge 30 minutes before beating them. This mousse freezes beautifully. Thaw it in the fridge for several hours before serving.

Classic Chocolate Mousse (Simple, But Not Foolproof)

1 STICK BUTTER

1 C. COCOA

12 EGGS

½ C. HEAVY CREAM OR MILK

DASH SALT

3 C. SUGAR

1–2 TBSP. EXTRACT OF YOUR CHOICE: VANILLA, ALMOND, OR MINT

½ TSP. CREAM OF TAR-TAR

1 PINT HEAVY WHIPPING CREAM

IN A MEDIUM SAUCEPAN, melt the butter and cocoa over low heat. In two separate containers, separate the eggs; keep 10 of the yolks and all of the whites. Whisk the yolks, ½ C. cream or milk, and salt. Whisk the egg mixture into the fully melted butter/cocoa mixture, still over low heat. If it begins to thicken, remove from heat immediately and keep whisking. Using a wooden spoon, continue to stir over low heat; add 2 C. sugar. The mixture will seem too thick at first, but keep on stirring until it becomes smooth. Stir in the last 1 C. sugar until smooth. Remove from heat and mix in your choice of extract. Allow the chocolate mixture to cool to room temperature; this is done most quickly by putting it into the fridge for about 20 minutes, stirring it and scraping the sides every 5 minutes. In your biggest metal mixing bowl, beat the 12 egg whites and cream of tartar. Whip until stiff, but not dry, peaks form. In another bowl, beat the whipping cream until it's fluffy and firm. Stir 1 C. of the cooled chocolate mixture into the whipped cream. Carefully fold the rest of the chocolate mixture into the whipped cream, making a chocolate cream. Drizzle about one-fourth of the chocolate cream across the top of the egg whites. Very carefully and thoroughly fold it in. Repeat, using one-fourth of the chocolate mixture at a time, until all the chocolate cream is incorporated into the whites. Pour gently into storage containers. Chill for several hours before serving.

Men come and go, but chocolate is forever.

"It has been shown as proof positive that carefully prepared chocolate is as healthful a food as it is pleasant; that it is nourishing and easily digested . . . that it is above all helpful to people who must do a great deal of mental work."
—Anthelme Brillat-Savarin

This is easy-peasy. Some people call this type of recipe a mousse, but to me it's not fluffy enough to be considered a true mousse—it's delicious, but to me it's a pudding. The level of richness will be determined by the type of chocolate you use—whether it's milk or semi-sweet. The latter makes a much stronger, richer flavor. The recipe doesn't make a huge batch—just enough to satisfy a family's sweet tooth with small portions . . . or one or two people's serious need for a chocolate fix (if you can wait a few hours while it chills, that is—larger portions take longer to set).

Easy Chocolate Pudding

1 C. WHIPPING CREAM

1 C. CHOCOLATE CHIPS

1 EGG

¼ C. SUGAR

¼ TSP. SALT

2 TBSP. AMARETTO FLAVORING OR 1 TSP. ALMOND EXTRACT

IN A SMALL SAUCEPAN, bring the whipping cream to a boil. (If you have a "sure simmer" setting on your microwave, use that instead and set it for 15 seconds of simmering). While the whipping cream is heating, pour the remaining ingredients into a blender. Transfer the hot cream to a Pyrex measuring cup with a spout. Turn on the blender and very slowly drizzle the simmering cream in a thin stream into the blender. Let the mixture blend for another few seconds until smooth. Pour into a glass bowl or demitasse serving cups. Chill for at least an hour. Garnish with whipped cream and a chocolate-dipped strawberry. Or do what I do: grab a spoon and dig in!

Chocolate is nature's way of making up for Mondays.

This ice cream has a rich, chocolate flavor that's to die for. You can always tweak it so it has less cocoa and isn't quite so rich, but then I'd have to consider you a wimp.

Classic Chocolate Ice Cream

3 C. MILK

3 C. WHIPPING CREAM

2 TBSP. VANILLA

2 C. SUGAR

1 TSP. SALT

1 C. COCOA

TAKE THE MILK and whipping cream out of the fridge an hour or more before you make the ice cream so they can reach room temperature; this allows the sugar to dissolve more easily, making the final product much smoother and better. (As an alternate, you can mix the milk and whipping cream in a large bowl and microwave for 2–4 minutes to warm them up slightly.) Combine the lukewarm milk, whipping cream, and vanilla. In a medium bowl, sift the sugar, salt, and cocoa. Add to the whipping cream mixture. Beat for about 2 minutes or until the sugar is completely dissolved and the mixture is smooth. Pour into the ice cream maker canister and freeze according to manufacturer's instructions. Note: If you have only a pint of whipping cream on hand, you can use half-and-half instead of milk; use 2 C. whipping cream and replace the milk with 2 C. half-and-half.

There are four basic food groups—milk, dark, white, and bittersweet...

My kids love this classic ice cream; it's hard to put too many cookies into it (except that the ice cream canister holds only so much . . .). Here's my secret weapon: To create a nice, creamy texture in ice cream, make sure the sugar is fully dissolved. The best way I've found to do that is to warm up the cream and milk just a tad before stirring in the sugar. I don't get it very warm, but the sugar dissolves much quicker and easier if the cream and milk aren't cold from the fridge—and the finished ice cream is creamier.

Cookies and Cream Ice Cream

4 C. (1 QT.) WHIPPING CREAM

3 C. MILK

2 C. SUGAR

1 TSP. SALT

2 TSP. VANILLA

2–3 C. SANDWICH-STYLE COOKIES (SUCH AS OREOS), ROUGHLY CHOPPED INTO FOURTHS

IN A LARGE, microwave-safe bowl, combine all ingredients except the cookies. Cook on high for about 5 minutes. (Alternately, you can cook the ingredients in a large pot on the stove for a few minutes to reduce the chill.) Stir the mixture with a wooden spoon until the sugar is fully dissolved and integrated. Add the cookies. Pour the mixture into the ice cream maker canister, making sure it doesn't come above the manufacturer's fill line. Freeze according to the manufacturer's directions. To cure and harden the ice cream, put it into the freezer for a couple of hours before serving. Tip: In a typical pack of Oreos, one "sleeve" of cookies chopped into fourths equals 2 C. If you want 3 C., use half of another sleeve; 3 C. will yield a very cookie-flavored and chocolate-looking ice cream!

Grasshopper Ice Cream Variation: Use no more than 2 C. chopped cookies. Add 10–20 drops green food coloring. Replace the vanilla extract with 1 tsp. mint extract.

I have only two words to describe this one: easy and YUM! Biting into chunks of chocolate-covered cherries in the middle of your chocolate ice cream is about as close to pure bliss as you can get.

Chocolate Cherry Cordial Ice Cream

2 C. MILK

2 C. WHIPPING CREAM

2½ C. SUGAR

¼ –⅓ C. COCOA, AS DESIRED

2 TBSP. VANILLA

½ TSP. SALT

1 12-OZ. CAN EVAPO-RATED MILK

12–18 CHOCOLATE-COVERED CHERRIES (SEE NOTE)

IN A LARGE BOWL, combine milk, whipping cream, sugar, cocoa, and vanilla; use a whisk to incorporate the cocoa if necessary. Micro-wave for 2–3 minutes or warm the mixture on the stove slightly to remove the chill and to help the sugar dissolve fully so the ice cream won't be grainy. You don't want the mixture warm; it should just not be cold. Add the salt and evaporated milk. Mix well. Pour the mix-ture into the freezing container; if the cocoa isn't completely mixed in, pour the mixture through a sieve into the freezing container so you don't end up with cocoa bits in the ice cream. Freeze in an ice cream maker according to manufacturer's instructions. Ap-proximately halfway through freezing, turn off the machine and remove the lid; cut up the chocolate-covered cherries with scissors and add them to the thickening ice cream. Continue freezing until

Without chocolate, there would be darkness and chaos.

90

Chocolate: Not against the Word of Wisdom. Yet...

finished. Store the ice cream in an airtight container. If you can wait to eat it (good luck with that), put the ice cream in the freezer for a couple of hours to firm it up.

Note: If you have actual chocolate-covered cordial cherries on hand, use those. If not, half a 16-oz. bottle of maraschino cherries will do the trick. Melt 1 C. semisweet chocolate chips, drop each cherry into the chocolate, roll it around with a soup spoon to coat, and dry on waxed or parchment paper. To firm the cherries up faster, put them on a cookie sheet and chill in the fridge.

In chocolate's early years, it was available only to nobility. The regular folk (who frankly could have used some chocolate in their stressful daily lives) had no access to it.
All that changed with the world's first chocolate shop, which opened in London in 1657.
At that point, solid chocolate treats weren't available, so it was consumed as a drink.
Nearly 350 years later, the craving masses haven't looked back. We raise our mugs of hot chocolate in gratitude.

This is recipe is essentially homemade ice cream sandwiches on steroids. They take a little time, but they're really easy, and the end result is so worth it. The chocolate cookie part is rich, so while you can use any kind of ice cream for the filling, I recommend starting out with vanilla to balance out the intensity of the chocolate. That way, you won't give yourself a chocolate hangover the first time around. You can always try the recipe again and fill it with Burnt Almond Fudge, Rocky Road, or something equally chocolaty.

Ice Cream Sandwich Stacks

2 STICKS BUTTER

1 C. SUGAR

1 C. BROWN SUGAR

2 EGGS

1 TSP. VANILLA

3½ C. FLOUR

¾ C. COCOA

1 TSP. BAKING SODA

½ GALLON VANILLA (OR OTHER FLAVOR) ICE CREAM

PREHEAT OVEN TO 375. Line a 9 x 13 glass pan with foil, with several inches hanging over the ends like "handles"; coat with nonstick spray. Cream butter and sugars; add eggs and vanilla. Mix well. Add flour, cocoa, and baking soda. Mix until well combined. Divide the dough into four sections. Press one section of the dough into a single layer in the pan as evenly as you can. Bake for about 12 minutes. Remove the chocolate cookie layer, using the foil "handles" to lift it out of the pan; cool on a wire rack or cookie sheet. Repeat with two more sections of the dough: line the pan with foil, spray, and press the dough into a layer. Bake for 12 minutes. Remove by the extra foil "handles" and cool. (Note: As the dish progressively heats, you may need to bake each layer for less time; watch carefully to avoid over-baking.) For the final section of dough, coat the pan with nonstick spray and press the dough directly into the pan; don't use foil. As the final of the four layers is cooling in the pan,

Hand over the chocolate and no one gets hurt

remove the ice cream from the freezer and allow it to soften for about 15 minutes, just enough so you can scoop it out and spread it. When the layers are completely cooled, spread ice cream over the first layer. Top with another cookie layer; spread with ice cream; top with another cookie layer; spread with ice cream; and top with the final cookie layer. Cover with foil or plastic wrap and put the entire dish back into the freezer to harden for about an hour. (If you need to leave it longer than hour, take it out of the freezer about half an hour before serving so it can soften a bit before cutting.) Cut into slices with a hot, wet knife. Whether with your hands or a fork, enjoy three layers of cookie and two of ice cream!

Chocolate confession from Karen:
I have always loved chocolate, but in the past few years I found out that chocolate is a trigger for my migraines. Faced with having to choose between chocolate and dealing with debilitating headaches, there was really only one choice: CHOCOLATE! Hey, I can live with a migraine. I can't live without chocolate.

I could give up chocolate, but I'm no quitter.

The amazing part of this one—it's healthy. Seriously. Especially if you use dark chocolate. This concept has been popular on blogs; word has it that Naomi Poe first figured out the secret. The versions I first found had funky measurements, so I sort of winged it. My version had my kids literally singing praises: my youngest did a little hallelujah angel-like chorus thing. The amazing thing is how the stuff not only stays liquid at room temperature for days on end, but how it freezes up just like the old magic shell after hitting ice cream. It does eventually harden up, in which case, simply warm it up under tap water or put it in the microwave for a bit, and—voila!—perfect Magic Shell again.

Magic Shell for Ice Cream

2 C. CHOCOLATE CHIPS

1 C. COCONUT OIL (FOUND IN THE COOKING OIL SECTION OF YOUR HEALTH-FOOD STORE)

⅛ TSP. SALT

IN A SMALL PYREX BOWL, heat the combined ingredients in the microwave for about 1 minute. Mix with a rubber scraper, then heat for another minute. Repeat at 30-second intervals until the mixture is mostly melted, but not quite. Remove and stir, letting the heat of the mixture and the bowl melt the rest of it. When the mixture is completely melted, use a funnel to pour it into a plastic squeeze bottle. Pour over a bowl of ice cream and watch it freeze like, well, magic before you dig in. Store at room temperature. Note: Be sure the bottle you store the Magic Shell in is totally clean and (especially!) dry. Water—even a drop or two—can ruin the chemistry of the chocolate.

Here's a fun bit of physics: What happens when you add warm, melted chocolate to freshly frozen ice cream? The chocolate freezes on contact, turning into shards of delicious goodness. That's the concept behind this recipe. The base is white chocolate, vanilla, banana, and coconut (hence the "crazy monkey" part). I like to add candied cashews as well. You really can play with it, adding or subtracting ingredients. But the best part is at the end when you add the melted chocolate to the freshly frozen ice cream and get long, yummy pieces of chocolate floating in your ice cream. Oh, yeah . . .

Crazy Monkey Ice Cream

½ C. WHITE CHOCO-LATE CHIPS

2 C. MILK

2 C. WHIPPING/HEAVY CREAM

1 TBSP. VANILLA

⅓ C. SUGAR

3 MEDIUM RIPE BA-NANAS, MASHED

½ C. COCONUT, GRAT-ED OR SHREDDED

½ C. CANDIED CA-SHEWS, CHOPPED (SEE NOTE)

½ C. CHOCOLATE CHIPS (MILK OR SEMI-SWEET)

2 TSP. OIL

MELT THE WHITE CHOCOLATE CHIPS; add a little oil or nonstick spray if needed to make the chips liquid. Set aside. In a large pan, combine the milk, cream, vanilla, and sugar; heat on low. When the mixture is warm (not hot) and the sugar has dissolved, add the melted white chocolate chips (this keeps the white chocolate from hardening). Remove from heat. Add the bananas and coconut. Pour the mixture into the freezing canister and freeze according to the manufacturer's directions. When finished, remove the canister and stir in the cashews. Melt the chocolate chips. With a spoon or rubber scraper, drizzle a small amount of the melted chips over the top of the ice cream. Immediately stir, letting the chocolate freeze into the ice cream. Repeat with several small drizzle amounts until the chocolate is gone, being sure to stir up the bottom of the canister so chocolate shards are mixed throughout the ice cream. Put

I tried a dessert called, "Death by Chocolate," but it only made me stronger.

the lid on the canister and freeze for several hours so the ice cream can fully harden before serving.

Note: To make candied cashews, use a large knife to chop the cashews. Cover a cookie sheet with a layer of parchment and spread the cashews across it. Sprinkle a couple of tablespoons of brown sugar over the nuts. Using a spatula—or even just your hands—mix well. Bake at 350 for 4–6 minutes, stirring well halfway through. Let cool thoroughly before using in a recipe.

Chocolate isn't just candy anymore. It's a lifestyle

Wheat is for man. D&C 89:19
Chocolate is for woman. M&M 24:7

This is a frozen, mousselike dessert to die for. Unlike what the name suggests, it doesn't grow in the freezer, but it is fluffy like a soufflé—and, of course, it's much more enjoyable than, say, a spinach soufflé. (I grew up on those and did enjoy them, Mom. But you know chocolate wins out, right?)

Frozen Chocolate Soufflé

1 C. + 3½ C. HALF-AND-HALF

5 TBSP. CORNSTARCH

¼ C. COCOA

1 C. SUGAR + ½ C. SUGAR

2 TSP. VANILLA

1 TSP. HAZELNUT OIL, ALMOND EXTRACT, MINT EXTRACT, OR OTHER FLAVORING OF YOUR CHOICE

¾ C. SEMISWEET CHOCOLATE, CHIPS OR CHOPPED

5 EGG WHITES

⅛ TSP. SALT

WHITE CHOCOLATE BAR FOR GARNISH (OPTIONAL)

IN A 2-CUP LIQUID MEASURING CUP, combine 1 C. of the half-and-half, the cornstarch, and the cocoa; mix until smooth. Set aside. In a medium saucepan, combine the remaining 3½ C. half-and-half, 1 C. of the sugar, the vanilla, and the hazelnut oil or other flavoring. Heat almost to a simmer, stirring frequently; don't let the mixture boil. Once the mixture has nearly reached a simmer, pour the cold half-and-half mixture from the measuring cup into the pan and whisk constantly. Reduce the heat so it won't set up or thicken too fast at the base. When the mixture is almost puddinglike in consistency, remove from heat and add the chocolate, whisking until the chocolate is completely incorporated. Set aside and allow the mixture to cool to room temperature. In a large bowl, beat the egg whites and salt until you have medium peaks that are starting to get glossy. While still beating, gradually add the remaining ½ C. sugar, a couple of tablespoons at a time. Beat until very stiff

"Stressed" spelled backward is "desserts." Coincidence? I think not.

peaks form, but be careful not to over-beat—the whites shouldn't get dry. Fold the cooled chocolate mixture into the whites, about ¾ C. at a time; fold carefully so the whites keep their loft. When the chocolate and the whites are completely integrated, pour the mixture into either three glass loaf pans or about a dozen 1-cup custard cups. Freeze until solid (at least 6–7 hours for the loaf pans, less time for the cups). Serve from the loaf pans with an ice cream scoop. If desired, garnish with curls from the white chocolate bar; shave the chocolate with a vegetable peeler and pile the curls on top of each serving.

In one of its weight-loss articles, Reader's Digest *wrote that the average craving lasts only ten minutes.*
I find that mine last much shorter than that. I mean, really, how long does it take to get the wrapper off an Almond Joy?
—Janette Rallison, author of My Fair Godmother
and many other young-adult novels

When my second daughter—who declares she's spent years trying to like pie with no success—saw this one, her eyes turned into wide saucers, and she immediately said, "Um, Mom, I think I'll like this pie." This variation on a classic is easy to make, but creating all three major components—the crust, the ice cream, and the fudge sauce—can be time-consuming. You can simplify the process by buying them all. Personally, I think you should shoot for making at least one or two from scratch, since it really will taste better. They're all easy but take time and effort—so making all three from scratch should grant you sainthood.

Mississippi Mud Pie

1–1½ QUARTS OF YOUR FAVORITE CHOCOLATE-BASED ICE CREAM

FROM THIS BOOK, YOU CAN MAKE:

MINT CHOCOLATE CHIP ICE CREAM (P. 83)

CLASSIC CHOCOLATE ICE CREAM (P. 88)

CHOCOLATE CHERRY CORDIAL ICE CREAM (P. 90)

COOKIES AND CREAM ICE CREAM (P. 89)

Ingredients continued on next page.

LET THE ICE CREAM SOFTEN A BIT, either by leaving it at room temperature about half an hour or by softening it in the microwave for several 30-second intervals at half power. Scoop ½ C. fudge sauce into the pie crust and smooth evenly with a spoon (tip: spray the measuring cup with nonstick spray so the sticky sauce will easily slide out). Be careful not to destroy the bottom of the crust; since the fudge is so sticky, it's very easy to inadvertently start lifting up entire sections of the crust, resulting in holes. Spoon half the ice cream over the fudge sauce; spread evenly. Spoon another ½ C. fudge sauce over the ice cream, bringing the fudge only to within a quarter inch of the edges. Scoop the rest of the ice cream over the second layer of sauce, bringing the ice cream completely to the edges so the fudge underneath doesn't show. Top with the remaining ½ C. fudge sauce. Sprinkle with nuts or toffee bits. Freeze the pie until the ice cream and fudge sauce are both hardened,

100

If I can't have too many truffles, I'll do without. —Colette

1 CHOCOLATE-COOKIE CRUMB CRUST (P. 104), BAKED AND COOLED

1½ C. HOT FUDGE SAUCE (P. 172), COOLED

½ C. NUTS (ALMONDS, WALNUTS, OR PECANS), CHOPPED, OR TOFFEE BITS (LIKE HEATH BITS)

WHIPPED CREAM FOR GARNISH

about an hour. Serve immediately or put into a large zip-style bag or cover tightly with plastic wrap to protect it from freezer burn for a few more days. If the pie will be in the freezer for several hours, take it out about twenty-five minutes before serving so it can soften a bit. To help cut it, run a knife under hot water before making each slice. Serve with dollops of whipping cream.

"Ugh! They insulted chocolate!"
—My oldest daughter at the age of nine,
on seeing a commercial for a new
"chocolate" cell phone,
which (the nerve!) wasn't even brown

My mother-in-law has a Danish background, and to keep some of that culture alive, she makes these at Christmas. She fills them with cherry pie filling, too, but the most popular filling each year is—no surprise—the chocolate filling. One year for my birthday, she gave me a set of tart tins and her recipes. Now I make them for my kids each Christmas. Instead of mini tart shells, you can use silicon molds, mini muffin tins, or other small forms. I've personally used only the actual tart tins, but my mother-in-law has reported success using all kinds of other things.

Chocolate Danish Mini Tarts

TART SHELLS:

1 C. BUTTER

1 C. + 1 TBSP. SUGAR

1 EGG

½ TSP. ALMOND EXTRACT

2½–2¾ C. FLOUR

CHOCOLATE TART FILLING:

8 OZ. MILK CHOCOLATE*

18 LARGE MARSHMALLOWS

½ C. MILK

1 C. WHIPPING CREAM

PREHEAT OVEN TO 350. Shells: Lightly coat tart tins with cooking spray. Cream butter and sugar. Add egg and almond extract. Mix in flour as needed to make the dough moist but not sticky. It should be workable with your hands. Work small amounts of dough into individual tart tins. You'll need less than you think; they should not have thick bottoms. Prick each shell with a fork a couple of times, then bake for about 10 minutes, until barely golden on the edges. Let cool, then remove from tins and fill. Makes about 24 shells, depending on size. Filling: In a medium pan, melt the chocolate, marshmallows, and milk. Allow the mixture to cool completely to room temperature. Whip the cream and then fold it into the chocolate mixture until fully incorporated, with no chocolate streaks. Fill shells (this is easiest with the zip-bag trick; see p. 7). Chill filled tarts for about an hour before serving. Garnish with a squirt of whipped cream.

*My mother-in-law often uses simple Hershey's bars. I like to use Guittard milk chocolate chips, the giant ones in the silver bag.

Chocolate-Cookie Crumb Crust

2½ C. CHOCOLATE COOKIE PIECES WITHOUT CREAM FILLING (SEE NOTE)

6 TBSP. BUTTER, MELTED

1 EGG WHITE

PREHEAT OVEN TO 350. Put the cookie pieces into a blender and blend, with the lid on, for 30 seconds or so. Turn off and shake, lid still on, so larger cookie pieces and crumbs are distributed. Blend again to get the larger pieces broken up. (I've tried this in my food processor, but the blender worked better.) While still blending, add the melted butter and then the egg white. Don't worry if the entire mixture isn't moist. Dump into a 9-inch pie dish and use a spoon to finish mixing it so everything gets moistened. Using your fingers, spread the crust evenly along the base and edges of the pie dish. Bake for 10–12 minutes or until set. Allow to cool completely before filling. If using a glass dish (recommended for chilled desserts like French Silk Pie), you can put the dish into the fridge for about 15 minutes and then move it to the freezer to help it cool faster, but never put a glass dish straight from the oven into the freezer; it will shatter. Note: Chocolate graham crackers, such as Teddy Grahams, work well (a heaping 2-cup Pyrex measuring cup is about perfect, which is about half of a 10-ounce bag). Don't use chocolate cookies with cream filling (such as Oreos)—you want plain chocolate cookies that will yield pure crumbs, not additional cream or fat.

Variation: If you want to make a cookie crumb crust from scratch, use the Chocolate Shortbread Cookies recipe (p. 42). Use 10–12 of these cookies for the crust. Because they're softer than graham crackers, mash them with a fork or rolling pin; they tend to clog the blender because of the extra moisture.

....There's nothing wrong with me that a little chocolate won't cure.........

Sweet chocolate story from Mary Jane:
I have three-year-old twins, and one of them is a total chocolate
lover. They were premature, and when they turned one month old,
I brought in chocolate cupcakes for the nurses. They let me put the
smallest dot of frosting on my little babies' lips. That was my sons'
first real food. I think that is why they love chocolate so much now!

Depending on the chocolate you use, these can have an intense chocolate pudding flavor. For adults who like intense chocolate, semisweet chocolate is awesome. For kids who crinkle their noses at intense chocolate and prefer the lighter stuff, definitely use milk chocolate. Either way, these pops are utterly creamy—an easy, delicious recipe that's perfect for those summer chocolate cravings. The hardest part is waiting for the pops to freeze. So when I'm a big hurry, instead of freezing big pops, I use ice-cube trays. They freeze faster, and then I can pop one bite-size piece of bliss into my mouth after another!

Fudge Pudding Pops

2 C. + 2 TBSP. MILK (I PREFER WHOLE MILK, BUT 2% AND 1% WORK TOO)

¾ C. SUGAR

1 C. CHOCOLATE, CHOPPED OR IN CHIPS

3 EGG YOLKS

2 TBSP. CORNSTARCH

1 TBSP. BUTTER

½ TSP. VANILLA

IN A HEAVY SAUCEPAN, combine 2 C. milk and the sugar. Bring to a boil, stirring regularly until the sugar is dissolved. Reduce to simmer. Whisk in the chocolate until it is completely melted. In a small bowl, whisk the egg yolks. Add 2–3 Tbsp. of the chocolate mixture to the yolks; whisk well to combine, then immediately add them to the rest of the chocolate mixture and whisk to combine. In another small bowl, whisk the remaining 2 Tbsp. milk and the cornstarch. Slowly whisk the cornstarch mixture into the hot chocolate mixture. Bring to a boil and cook, stirring constantly, until thick. Remove from heat. Stir in the butter and vanilla. Using either a container with a spout or the zip-bag trick (see p. 7), pour the chocolate mixture into plastic popsicle molds. Add the lids and put into the freezer. (Note: Instead of regular molds, you can also use disposable plastic cups; after filling, cover the tops with foil and insert wooden popsicle sticks, using the foil to hold the sticks vertical. You can also use other molds to freeze the mixture, such as ice-cube trays.) Put into the freezer immediately and allow them to set for several hours or until hard. To remove from molds, run the outside of the mold under warm water to help loosen the pop.

I'd never attempted a bread pudding recipe before inventing this one, but when someone insisted I include a chocolate bread pudding recipe, I figured I'd better oblige . . . and figure out how to. I did a bunch of research, found several chocolate versions, and then decided to wing it and invent my own based on the kinds of things I'd seen. I have to say it turned out pretty darn good—but that's probably because it was the one of the last recipes I experimented with, so by that point, I was less of a kitchen novice than I had been four months prior. There's something to be said for intense learning curves.

Chocolate Bread Pudding

10 OZ. (APPROXIMATE-LY) DAY-OLD FRENCH BREAD (OR OTHER GOOD-QUALITY BAKERY BREAD), CUT INTO BITE-SIZE CHUNKS

1 C. SEMISWEET CHOCO-LATE CHIPS, MELTED

1 C. WHIPPING CREAM

1 C. CHOCOLATE MILK

2 EGGS

⅛ TSP. SALT

1 TSP. VANILLA

½ C. ALMONDS, SLICED (OPTIONAL)

BUTTER A 7 X 11-INCH GLASS DISH. Toss the bread chunks into a large mixing bowl and set aside. In a separate bowl, mix melted chocolate chips, whipping cream, and chocolate milk. In a small bowl, lightly beat the eggs, salt, and vanilla with a fork. Add to the chocolate mixture and beat. Spoon enough of the chocolate mixture into the dish to just cover the bottom. Add half of the bread cubes. Spoon half of the remaining chocolate mixture over the cubes, pressing them down to make sure they all touch the sauce. Repeat, adding the last of the cubes and the last of the chocolate sauce. Push the bread down gently in spots so it all touches the chocolate sauce. Let the pudding soak for at least half an hour; you can even cover the dish with plastic wrap and let it soak overnight. (Remove the dish from the fridge and let it warm up half an hour before baking.) Preheat the oven to 350. Right before baking, sprinkle the almonds over the top. Bake for 35–40 minutes, until the top is set. Serve warm or cold. Ice cream is a nice side, as is chocolate syrup drizzled over the top.

I attempted a few versions before landing on a French silk pie that was simply divine. One similar recipe I found had only three squares of baking chocolate in it. Chocolate-wise, it was utterly anemic. Three ounces of chocolate in a French silk pie? You call that a chocolate pie? On what planet? Mine has two cups of chocolate chips—roughly twelve ounces (four times that of other recipes' sad attempts). I'm sorry, but anything less than that is just plain wrong for a nine-inch dessert claiming to be chocolate.

French Silk Pie

FILLING:

1 C. MILK CHOCOLATE CHIPS

1 C. SEMISWEET CHOCO-LATE CHIPS

1 STICK BUTTER

1 TSP. VANILLA

1 C. POWDERED SUGAR

3 EGGS (REMOVE FROM FRIDGE 15–30 MINUTES PRIOR TO USE TO WARM UP SLIGHTLY SO THEY'LL BEAT BETTER)

1 9-INCH CHOCOLATE-COOKIE CRUMB CRUST (P. 104)

WHIPPED CREAM FOR GARNISH

USING THE CHOCOLATE MELTING GUIDELINES, (see pp. 5–7), melt the milk chocolate and semisweet chocolate chips, mixing well. Set aside. In a large mixing bowl, beat butter until fluffy. Add vanilla and powdered sugar. Beat until well-mixed, scraping edges of bowl as necessary. Add the melted chocolate and mix well. One at a time, add the eggs, beating the mixture for at least two full minutes on medium-high to high speed after each egg. Spread the filling evenly into cool pie crust. Chill for several hours before serving. I like to use glass pie dishes for chilled desserts, because the glass holds the cold better than metal does. Serve each slice with a dollop of whipped cream. For an extra wow effect, add a bit of grated chocolate on top and a drizzle of chocolate syrup.

CAUTION: This recipe contains raw eggs, which, in rare cases, may contain salmonella bacteria and can lead to food poisoning. Be sure to practice safe food-handling practices (wash the eggs, keep them in the fridge prior to use,

...Chocolate: The breakfast of champions. ...

don't let the final pie sit out for extended periods). Raw eggs can be a real health concern, especially for people with weakened immune systems. As an alternative, you can make this recipe using pasteurized egg product found at grocery stores in the dairy section. Such products explain how much of the product equals one egg and how to use them in place of raw eggs.

Everything I eat should contain either garlic or chocolate, but rarely both.

*Emergency alert: If the wearer is found vacant,
listless, or depressed, administer chocolate immediately.
(found on a T-shirt)*

So easy to make, so hard to wait for—because to get the best results on this one, you'll want to let it set up in the freezer for at least eight hours, or preferably overnight. For a chocoholic, that's a killer wait. (Licking the bowl can help pass part of the time.) But if you plan ahead, the pie is worth every long-awaited, delectable bite.

Chocolate Mint Pie

1 C. WHIPPING CREAM

¼ C. POWDERED SUGAR

4 OZ. UNSWEETENED BAKING CHOCOLATE, MELTED

1 CAN SWEETENED CONDENSED MILK

1 TSP. PEPPERMINT EXTRACT

1 8-INCH COOKIE CRUST (CHOCOLATE-COOKIE CRUMB OR GRAHAM CRACKER CRUSTS BOTH WORK WELL)

WHIP THE CREAM until it's light and fluffy. Add the powdered sugar and mix in on low so the cream doesn't continue to whip. In a separate bowl, blend the melted chocolate with the sweetened condensed milk. Stir in the whipped cream and peppermint extract. Pour the mixture into the pie crust and freeze for at least 8 hours or overnight before serving. The pie will be soft enough to cut, serve, and eat directly out of the freezer; there's no need to defrost first.

I found several recipes with this name. To my horror, the only way any of them differed from regular pecan pie was the addition of chocolate chips. To me, that wasn't nearly enough of a change to warrant an entirely new recipe. In my (always loud) chocoholic opinion, a true chocolate pecan pie needed a chocolate-based filling. The chocolate would be the point. Here, the pecans are chopped into small pieces, adding flavor and nutty goodness. It's seriously rich, but it's properly chocolaty. Serve warm or chilled, with vanilla ice cream on the side or a big dollop of whipped cream on top.

Chocolate Pecan Pie

CRUST:

1¼ C. FLOUR

½ TSP. SALT

⅓ C. + 1 TBSP. BUTTER

3–4 TBSP. ICE WATER

CHOCOLATE PECAN PIE FILLING:

1 STICK BUTTER

1 C. SUGAR

¾ C. CORN SYRUP

½ C. SEMISWEET CHOCOLATE CHIPS, MELTED

1 TSP. VANILLA

½ TSP. SALT

Ingredients continued on next page.

CRUST: CUT THE FLOUR, salt, and butter together with a pastry blender (or use two butter knives, pulling opposite one another through the mixture) until the butter pieces are the size of peas. Add the water, one tablespoon at a time, to form a dough that's workable with the hands and not too wet. Roll the dough into a ball and place on a floured counter; dust the top of the dough with flour. Dust a rolling pin with flour and gently roll the dough into a 9-inch circle. If the dough is too sticky, add more flour, but be careful—the more you handle the dough, the poorer quality pastry it will be. Sometimes you can simply use a spatula to release it from the countertop. Tip: An easy way to transfer the pie crust to the pie tin is to fold the circle in half and then in half again, making a triangle. Now you can easily lift it off the counter. Place the point of the triangle in the center of the tin and unfold the crust. Gently press the crust into place with your fingers and shape as needed.

Stress wouldn't be so hard to take if it were chocolate-covered.

4 EGGS

1 C. PECANS, CHOPPED

1 C. SEMISWEET CHOCO-
LATE CHIPS

Filling: Preheat oven to 350. In a small saucepan over low to medium heat, melt the butter, sugar, and corn syrup, stirring constantly so they don't burn. When the ingredients are fully combined, remove from the heat and stir in the melted chocolate chips. Pour the mixture into a large mixing bowl. Add vanilla and salt; mix well. Add the eggs, one at a time, beating each until fully incorporated before adding the next one. Finally, stir in the pecans and chocolate chips. Pour the filling into the unbaked pie crust. Bake for about an hour, until the center is nearly set and no longer wobbles like liquid when gently shaken. Cool on a wire rack. If desired, chill for several hours before serving.

Who's gonna turn down a Junior Mint?
It's chocolate, it's peppermint, it's delicious.
—Cosmo Kramer, from the television series Seinfeld

This recipe is a classic case of "easy does not necessarily mean fast." You'll totally wow your guests with it, but you can't whip it up in half an hour. Baking takes a good hour and chilling several more. When it's time to wow the guests, it takes just moments to pull the chilled ramekins out of the fridge, sprinkle brown sugar over the tops, broil them to perfection, present them to a willing audience, and revel in their praise. When you say, "Oh, it was nothing," they won't realize that it really was nothing. Note: For this recipe, you'll need eight oven-safe ramekin cups that each hold four ounces (½ cup).

Chocolate Crème Brûlée

¾ C. SEMISWEET CHOCO-LATE CHIPS

2 C. WHIPPING CREAM

⅓ C. SUGAR

4 EGG YOLKS

1 TSP. VANILLA

1 TSP. SALT

¼ C. (AT LEAST) BROWN SUGAR

PREHEAT OVEN TO 300. Fill a 9 x 13 baking dish halfway with water. Depending on the shape of your ramekin dishes, you may need an additional smaller dish as well, also filled halfway with water. Put the water bath dish(es) into the oven on the center rack. In a large bowl, melt the chocolate chips until they're smooth. Stir in the cream and sugar. If the chocolate starts to separate into flecks, reheat it slightly. Reheat just until it's warm; be careful not to let the chocolate seize. Remove from heat and stir the mixture until it is smooth and well blended. Remove any white matter sticking to the egg yolks. Add the egg yolks, vanilla, and salt to the chocolate mixture and combine until smooth. Using a measuring cup, pour a scant ½ C. of the mixture into each of 8 oven-safe ramekin cups. Carefully open the oven and place the ramekins into the water bath. The water should come halfway up each cup. (If some of the water has already evaporated, add more, being careful not to let any splash into the cups.) Bake for 50–55 minutes, until the crème brûlées are set and a knife comes out nearly clean when inserted into the center. Remove and cool to room temperature. A slight skin may develop on the tops; that's normal. Refrigerate the cups for at least 3–4 hours. Do not cover the crème brûlées in the fridge, because this causes condensation (and remember that chocolate and water don't mix). Right before serving, remove the cups from the fridge and place on a baking sheet. Turn the oven onto broil and put the oven rack on the top position. Generously sprinkle brown sugar over the surface of each cup—a minimum of half a tablespoon, but preferably a bit more. Under the broiler's heat, the brown sugar will caramelize and turn almost candylike, so the more surface area it covers, the better the crust. Slide the cookie sheet with the cups directly under the broiling element. Keep a close eye on it, removing the baking sheet as soon as the brown sugar has melted and caramelized, which only takes 1–2 minutes. Be sure it doesn't burn. Serve immediately. Makes 8.

"Only 12 pounds? I obviously was not included in that survey."
—Tristi Pinkston, friend, fellow writer,
and chocoholic, commenting on a survey published
in the Los Angeles Times *stating*
that the average U.S. citizen consumes
12 pounds of chocolate annually

Snacks & Gifts

An easy fudge, another huge winner, and another one I have to be careful with—because if I don't watch it, I'll eat the whole pan and then gasp in horror when I realize exactly how much fat I just consumed. It's best to share this one with lots of people and cut it into many, many pieces.

Orange Fudge

1½ C. MILK CHOCO-LATE CHIPS

½ C. WHITE CHOCO-LATE CHIPS

1 TSP. OIL

½ STICK BUTTER

1 14-OZ. CAN SWEET-ENED CONDENSED MILK

1 TSP. ORANGE EX-TRACT

¼ C. TOFFEE BITS (SUCH AS HEATH BRAND)

¼ C. PECANS, CHOPPED

LINE AN 8 X 8 OR 9 X 9 SQUARE PAN with foil (heavy-duty is nice, but not necessary); let the foil hang over two opposite ends so you can use it as "handles" to remove the fudge later. Either coat the foil with nonstick spray or brush with butter. Set aside. Melt the milk chocolate chips, white chocolate chips, and oil together according to the guidelines (see pp. 5–7), mixing regularly. While still warm, add the butter and let the heat of the melted chocolate melt it. If it's not quite hot enough, reheat very slightly and briefly to melt the butter without seizing the chocolate. Once the butter is melted and mixed in, stir in the sweetened condensed milk and orange extract. When the mixture is smooth, pour it into the pan. Sprinkle the top with the toffee bits and nuts, then use your fingers to gently press them into the top of the fudge. Refrigerate for 3–4 hours to harden the fudge. Use the foil "handles" to lift the fudge out of the pan and onto a cutting board. Cut into 25 pieces—five rows by five rows. Makes a very rich and creamy—and delicious—fudge!

118

All I want is peace and love in the world. Okay, and chocolate.

For anyone who loves Hershey's Symphony bars (the ones in the blue wrapper with little toffee pieces), this recipe is awesome. After I made this one, my chocoholic daughter joked that she couldn't live without it—then quickly added, "Well, it's okay, I guess." For the next couple of days (miracle of miracles, it did last that long, probably because it was out of sight), she kept asking for another piece. "Not because I can't live without it," she'd say, "but because, you know, it's just okay . . ." and she'd grin. The next day when packing her school lunch, she packed extra pieces of the fudge so her friends could have a taste. Yeah, I think we have a winner.

"Symphonic" Peanut Butter Fudge

2 STICKS BUTTER

4 TBSP. COCOA

1 TSP. VANILLA

1 C. CREAMY PEANUT BUTTER

3 C. POWDERED SUGAR

1 LARGE HERSHEY'S SYMPHONY BAR (MILK CHOCOLATE OR TOFFEE), CHOPPED

LINE AN 8 X 8 OR 9 X 9 PAN with either parchment or a double layer of plastic wrap, leaving a few inches hanging over on both sides for "handles" that will help you easily remove the fudge from the pan after it hardens. Set aside. If using parchment, grease it well; if using plastic wrap, spray with nonstick spray. In a medium saucepan, melt the butter over low heat. Add cocoa and vanilla. Stir to blend. Turn off the burner and allow the remaining heat to keep the mixture warm (if you're using a gas stove, turn the burner to very low). Add peanut butter and stir until smooth. Add powdered sugar and continue stirring until the sugar is totally dissolved and the mixture is smooth. Pour the fudge mixture into the pan. Sprinkle the chocolate bar pieces over the top and spread evenly. The mixture will be thick. With clean fingers, press the chocolate pieces into the fudge, allowing the chocolate to sink down through the surface in places. Refrigerate for at least half an hour or until hardened. Use the "handles" of parchment or plastic wrap to remove the fudge from the pan; cut into 36 pieces (this is a very rich fudge!).

Quick and Easy Fudge

½ STICK BUTTER

1 14-OZ. CAN SWEET-ENED CONDENSED MILK

2 C. TOTAL (1 C. EACH) OF TWO DIFFERENT TYPES OF CHOCOLATE CHIPS

1 TSP. VANILLA EX-TRACT OR ½ TSP. ALMOND OR MINT EXTRACT

1 C. NUTS, CHOPPED

GREASE AN 8 X 8 SQUARE PAN. In a medium saucepan, melt the butter; stir in the milk. Remove from heat and stir in the chips. The heat of the milk and butter should melt the chips, but if you need more heat, put the pan back onto the stove briefly (take extreme care to not burn or scorch the chocolate). When the chocolate is completely melted, stir in the extract and nuts. Pour into the pan and smooth out evenly. Refrigerate until hard (about an hour). The fudge is very rich, so cut into small squares before serving.

Optional Marbling
After putting the fudge mixture into the pan, melt ½ C. white chocolate chips and drizzle the melted white chocolate over the top. Using a butter knife, make large S-curved shapes with the white chocolate into the fudge, creating a pretty marbled effect.

My Favorite Variation
For the chocolate, use half semisweet and half milk chocolate chips (preferably Guittard brand for both). Use almond extract (more than ½ tsp.), thinly sliced almonds, and white chocolate marbling.

This is an easy recipe that's fun to do with the kids. Feel free to play with it; it's hard to get wrong. See the notes below for some mouth-watering variations.

Chocolate Granola Bars

1 STICK BUTTER (PLUS A LITTLE EXTRA FOR GREASING THE DISH)

½ C. BROWN SUGAR

⅓ C. COCOA

2 C. BOXED GRANOLA CEREAL

1 TSP. VANILLA

½ C. CHOCOLATE CHIPS

½ C. PECANS, CHOPPED

LINE AN 11 X 7-INCH GLASS DISH with parchment; let the parchment hang over the edges a few inches as "handles" for easy removal. Grease the parchment with butter. In a large pot over medium heat, stir the butter, brown sugar, and cocoa until the butter is melted. Remove from heat. Stir in the granola, vanilla, chocolate chips, and pecans. Make sure the granola is evenly coated (break up chunks if necessary). Pour the mixture into the glass dish and smooth out the surface as best you can with a wooden spoon. Freeze for an hour or more, until nice and firm. (It's easier to cut into bars when cold.) Using the parchment "handles," lift the frozen granola bar block from the pan. Pull off the parchment and place the granola block onto a cutting board. Run a large knife under warm water, then use the heated blade to cut the block into 8 bars.

Awesome Granola Bar Variations:
—For a fun flavor kick, use a flavored granola, like a triple-berry crunch (you can never go wrong combining berries and chocolate).
—Instead of chopped pecans, use peanuts, walnuts, or almonds.
—Omit the nuts and replace them with ½ C. peanut butter chips.

These clusters of chocolate goodness are secretly good for your kids—so don't mention that fact as they gobble them down. In place of the cereal, you can use almost anything you have lying around. I use mini shredded wheat largely because it's whole-grain, but also because it's got a little more sweetness than something like plain old Cheerios—which is useful, since I use semisweet chips instead of milk chocolate. But you could use corn flakes, granola, or something else for the cereal. For that matter, you could try Craisins, dried apricots, or some other dried fruits in place of the dried cherries. Go crazy!

Chocolate Cherry Clusters

2 C. CHOCOLATE CHIPS (SEMISWEET OR MILK CHOCOLATE)

1½ C. LIGHTLY SMASHED SHREDDED MINI WHEATS OR OTHER HEALTHY CEREAL (SEE NOTE ABOVE)

1 6-OZ. PKG. DRIED CHERRIES

½ C. ALMONDS OR OTHER NUTS, CHOPPED

MELT THE CHOCOLATE in the microwave using the melting tips on pp. 5–7, being careful to not scorch the chocolate. Stir until smooth. Mix in the cereal, cherries, and nuts. Coat well. Drop by spoonfuls onto parchment and then refrigerate for a couple of hours until hardened. Enjoy!

To err is human, but to forgive, persuade me with chocolate.

These are a fun and easy variation of Chocolate Bark—without the crunchy topping that makes it "bark." The name comes from swirling the different chocolates and peanut butter mixture, creating the look of tiger stripes. Many claim these are a huge hit with guys. Since my guy isn't a peanut butter fan, I'll take their word for it.

Tiger Bites

1 LB. MILK CHOCOLATE

½ LB. WHITE CHOCOLATE

1 C. CREAMY PEANUT BUTTER (I PREFER ADAM'S)

COVER A BAKING SHEET with parchment. In separate glass bowls and using the guidelines for melting chocolate (see pp. 5–7), melt both chocolates either in the oven on very low heat or in the microwave. Stir each chocolate for two minutes to allow it to cool enough to prevent bloom. Spread the milk chocolate on the parchment in a rectangle ⅛ to ¼ inch thick. Add the peanut butter to the melted white chocolate; stir with a spoon until well combined. Drop the peanut butter mixture onto the milk chocolate in puddles. Drag a butter knife through the puddles and the milk chocolate to combine the two into whatever patterns you like— swirls, stripes, and so on. Allow the chocolate to set, either at room temperature (which will take much longer) or in the fridge (which takes much less time but risks the chance of bloom). When set, break into bite-size pieces and enjoy.

Tip: To measure the peanut butter, coat the measuring cup with a little non-stick spray before spooning in the peanut butter. The peanut butter will slip right out.

Once my youngest tasted chocolate milk, she refused to return to the white stuff. Naturally, for the sake of her bones, I absolutely must make chocolate milk for her on a regular basis. That's the kind of deep sacrifice mothers make. (Not that I drink any . . . ahem.)

Perfect Chocolate Milk

½ GAL. MILK (WE USE 1%)

⅓ C. SUGAR

⅓ C. COCOA

2 TSP. VANILLA

½ C. HAZELNUT-FLAVORED CREAMER, EITHER LIQUID OR POWDERED

POUR ONE QUART of milk into a pitcher; pour the other quart into a blender. Add the rest of the ingredients; blend well. Pour the milk from the blender into the pitcher; stir to mix. Makes just more than half a gallon of eye-rollingly delicious chocolate milk. Remember to stir again before each use in case any ingredients have settled since your last indulgence. Note: For a somewhat darker, richer chocolate milk, increase the cocoa to ½ C.

This is one of my favorite recipes. It's so easy yet packs a huge visual punch, and there are so many possiblities. We've made bark so often that my kids can do it alone. Once I almost forgot the birthday of a lady I visit teach, so I quickly made her a batch. She was stunned and amazed. I didn't have the heart to tell her that it took less time than chocolate chip cookies. Bark is layered chocolate, but for it to be "bark," it needs something crunchy on top: anything from nuts to nougat to crushed candy.

Chocolate Bark

3 DIFFERENT KINDS OF CHOCOLATE, PREFERABLY WITH CONTRASTING COLORS: 8 OZ. EACH OF 2 COLORS (ABOUT 1 C. IF YOU'RE USING CHIPS), AND 4 OZ. OF THE OTHER COLOR

EXAMPLES:

8 OZ. DARK CHOCOLATE AND MILK CHOCOLATE, 4 OZ. WHITE

8 OZ. MILK AND WHITE CHOCOLATE, 4 OZ. PINK

Ingredients continued on next page.

COVER A COOKIE SHEET with parchment. Melt each chocolate in a separate bowl in the order you'll be using the chocolate. (You can melt the first, then melt the second while you're using the first, and so on.) Pour the first melted chocolate onto the parchment. Using a rubber scraper or a butter knife, spread it into a rectangle on the parchment. Repeat with the second chocolate, spreading it on top of the first in a second layer. (If you'd like, leave a slight margin showing the color difference at the edge; you can also swirl the two colors together slightly to create a marbling pattern.) After melting the third chocolate, put it into a plastic bag and use the zip-bag trick (see p. 7) to drizzle the chocolate over the top in zigzags or other designs. Finish by sprinkling the crunchy item over the top. Refrigerate for about an hour so the chocolate can harden. When hardened, gently peel the Chocolate Bark off the parchment and break into bite-size pieces. Store in an airtight container.

8 OZ. DARK AND WHITE CHOCOLATE, 4 OZ. ORANGE

½ C. OR MORE NUTS, CRUSHED CANDY, OR OTHER CRUNCHY TOPPING

Note: You can find colored chocolate at specialty stores, or you can color it yourself with candy color—not food colorings or egg dyes—also available at specialty stores.

Note: The most common mistake when making Chocolate Bark is using chocolate that's too hot; this results in chocolate bloom and a bumpy, grainy texture. To prevent this, take a full minute or two to stir the chocolate before pouring each layer onto the parchment. This gets oxygen into the chocolate, tempering the chocolate crystals, resulting in gorgeous Chocolate Bark with a perfect texture and a glossy sheen.

*Strength is the capacity to break a chocolate bar
into four pieces with your bare hands
and then eat just one of the pieces. —Judith Viorst*

Avoid any diet that discourages the use of hot fudge. —Don Kardong

Whether you want to add a little zip as a garnish (say, to top off Tulip Cups filled with ice cream) or you just want a little bite-size bliss, Chocolate Meringue Kisses are the way to go. They're simple to make. The only hard part? Waiting. They take a long time to dry out in the oven. But the end result is worth it.

Chocolate Meringue Kisses

⅔ C. SUGAR

1½ C. POWDERED SUGAR

5 TBSP. COCOA

8 EGG WHITES

½ TSP. CREAM OF TAR-TAR

LINE 2–3 COOKIE SHEETS with parchment; set aside. Combine the sugar, powdered sugar, and cocoa. Sift. In a large mixing bowl, beat the egg whites and cream of tartar on high just until stiff (but not dry) peaks form. While still beating, gradually add the cocoa-sugar mixture, a few tablespoons at a time. Beat until the mixture is blended and the whites are firm and shiny. For the next step, you have a few options, depending on how fancy you want to get.

—If you have a pastry bag and a star tip, pipe pretty rosettes onto the parchment.

—Or, for most of us, fill a zip-style bag with the meringue, cut a corner off the bag, and pipe chocolate kisses with a pretty peaked top.

—Or use spoons to drop the mixture onto the parchment and form it into kiss shapes with a peak at the top.

Other things are just food. But chocolate's chocolate. —Patrick Skene Catling

Allow the kisses to rest for about 10 minutes. During that time, heat the oven to 220. Put the kisses into the oven for about 90 minutes. The point here is not to actually bake them but to dry them out. They shouldn't change color in the process. After 90 minutes, turn the oven off, leave the meringues in the oven, and let the oven cool completely. When the oven and the meringues are cool, take them out, gently remove them from the parchment with a spatula (they'll be fragile, so be careful not to break them), and store them in an airtight container. Use for garnishes (especially with ice cream!) or snacking. Makes several dozen, depending on size.

If you can't eat all your chocolate,
it will keep for months.
But if you can't eat all your chocolate,
what's wrong with you?

Molded Suckers & Mints

Gourmet Pretzel Rods

YOU'LL NEED:

JUMBO PRETZELS

A SOLID CARAMEL BLOCK

MELTING CHOCOLATE (SUCH AS GUITTARD A'PEELS)

EMBELLISHMENTS OF YOUR CHOICE, SUCH AS:

CONTRASTING COLOR(S) OF CHOCOLATE FOR DRIZZLE

TOFFEE BITS

CRUSHED CANDY CANES OR OTHER CANDY

CHOPPED NUTS

SPRINKLES

Cover a large area of the counter with parchment or waxed paper. Prepare your embellishments so they're ready to stick to the wet chocolate: put any sprinkles, nuts, crushed candy, or other embellishments onto plates so the pretzels can be rolled across them easily. Melt chocolate for drizzle and either put it in squeeze bottles or zip-style bags (see p. 10 for tricks on keeping the chocolate warm and liquid while you work).

Using a good knife (such as a butcher knife) and a cutting board, slice the caramel into pieces that measure about a quarter-inch or so thick. Then cut each of those slices into at least four or more pieces. Roll each piece of caramel into a "snake." When it's about a foot long, wrap it around a pretzel, starting at the top and spiraling it around, pressing gently so it attaches to the pretzel as it goes.

Come over to the dark side. We have chocolate.

The spiral should cover about two-thirds of the pretzel, leaving the last third empty. Repeat with all the pretzels you plan to dip.

Meanwhile, melt the chocolate in a large bowl. Stir the chocolate well periodically to keep it tempered and at the right temperature.

To coat the pretzel with chocolate easily, fill a tall glass about two-thirds with chocolate. Put a pretzel into the glass, then spoon chocolate over any of the caramel-covered part of the pretzel that doesn't have chocolate on it.

Let the excess chocolate drip off the pretzel (you can also wipe off the extra chocolate with the spoon). Immediately roll the pretzel into any toppings/embellishments and then lay it on the parchment or waxed paper. If you want to drizzle the pretzel with chocolate, do so now.

Repeat with remaining pretzels, refilling the glass with more chocolate as needed. Let the pretzels cool and harden before moving. They will likely puddle slightly, but no one minds extra chocolate! If desired, wrap in cellophane bags and tie with a ribbon.

Chocolate is cheaper than therapy and you don't need an appointment.

I had to do a Google search to be sure that the tails of zebras are striped just like the rest of them. Sure enough, they are. And while I think that zebras are white with black stripes, this recipe goes the other direction—but that just means the brown (and yummier) chocolate is more prominent than the less-yummy (white) chocolate. So I figure it all works out. It's great for a favor for birthday parties (especially any party with an animal or Noah's ark-type theme), especially since the kids can help make them!

Zebra or Tiger Tails

BAMBOO SKEWERS OR EXTRA-LONG (11¾-INCH) SUCKER STICKS

36 MARSHMALLOWS

3 C. SEMISWEET CHOCO-LATE CHIPS

¼ C. WHITE CHOCOLATE CHIPS

2 TBSP. VEGETABLE OIL + ½ TBSP. VEGETABLE OIL

SKEWER 4 MARSHMALLOWS onto each stick, lining the marshmallows up so they just reach the top. Melt the semisweet chocolate chips and 2 Tbsp. of the oil together until they're combined and thin enough for dipping. Spread enough parchment or waxed paper across your working surface to hold all of the skewers lying flat, with two inches between each one. (Alternately, place the parchment or waxed paper on a cookie sheet so you can put the Zebra Tails in the fridge to harden.) Dip each "tail" into the chocolate, using a spoon to scoop the chocolate so it covers the marshmallows completely. Gently remove any excess chocolate from the sides and bottom; the chocolate shouldn't be too thick. Place onto the parchment to harden. It's a good idea to stir the chocolate before dipping the marshmallows and between dipping each "tail" to be sure the chocolate cools and remains properly tempered. That way when it dries, the chocolate won't have bloom on it. Melt the white chocolate chips with ½ Tbsp. oil and stir until smooth. Using the zip-bag trick (see p. 7), drizzle across each dipped skewer, making zebra "stripes." Allow the chocolate to harden before eating or

134

putting into treat bags and tying off with a ribbon; refrigerating speeds this process considerably. Makes 9–10, depending on the thickness of the chocolate.

Variations:

—For a different look, use white chocolate as the base and semisweet chocolate for the stripes. Remember that unless you're using chocolate made for melting (not baking chips), you'll need to add more oil when using white chocolate.

—If you have access to a chocolate-supply store, use orange-colored and -flavored Guittard A'Peels for the base color and semisweet for the stripes, making Tiger Tails instead of Zebra Tails.

Las cosas claras y el chocolate espeso.
(Ideas should be clear and chocolate thick.)
—Spanish proverb

This recipe required a leap of faith for me to attempt: an actual candy recipe that takes a real candy thermometer? Yikes! Turns out it wasn't so scary after all. The biggest thing I learned is that it takes patience: you have to wait for the thermometer to reach the right temperature, you have to wait for the egg whites to reach the right stiffness, and you have to wait for the whites and syrup mixture to beat together long enough to make the divinity the right consistency. Patience is the key—something hard with chocolate, I know. But it's worth it. Take a look at some of the variations in the notes below. You can have some fun with this one.

Chocolate Divinity

3 C. SUGAR

¾ C. WATER

¾ C. LIGHT CORN SYRUP

¼ TSP. SALT

3 EGG WHITES

1 C. SEMISWEET CHOCOLATE CHIPS OR SEMISWEET CHOCOLATE, ROUGH-CHOPPED

ON THE COUNTERTOP, spread two or three long lengths of waxed paper. In a large, heavy saucepan, mix the sugar, water, corn syrup, and salt; cook over medium heat, stirring constantly, until the syrup comes to a boil, then stop stirring and continue to let the mixture boil until a candy thermometer reaches 250 degrees. Remove the pan from the heat. In a large bowl, beat the egg whites until soft (but not dry) peaks form. If possible, use a stand-alone mixer to make the process easier—a buddy also helps. Once the whites have soft peaks, gradually drizzle the hot syrup into the whites. Continue beating until the mixture begins to lose its gloss and hold a shape. At that point, quickly add the chocolate (and any other ingredients—see notes below). The mixture is hot, so the chocolate will melt on contact. Once it's all mixed together, use a spoon to quickly drop the divinity mixture onto the waxed paper; divinity cools quickly, so work rapidly. Allow to set. Another way to

To some people, it's a box of chocolate. To me, it's a support group.

finish it off is to press the divinity mixture into a greased, shallow 9 x 13 pan; allow to set before drizzling with chocolate and cutting into squares.

Variations: As you add the chocolate chips at the final stage of this recipe, you can also add other embellishments, including chopped nuts, such as hazelnuts, almonds, and pecans. Oils (not extracts) can add a great flavor to divinity as well (oils are usually not available at the grocery store).

—Hazelnut-Chocolate Divinity: For a great punch of flavor, use ¼ tsp. hazelnut oil and ½ C. chopped hazelnuts.

—Almond-Chocolate Divinity: Add almond oil and chopped almonds.

—Peppermint-Chocolate Divinity: Add ½ tsp. peppermint oil.

If not for chocolate, there would be no need for control-top pantyhose, and an entire industry would be devastated.

This recipe is so easy that including it in the book almost feels like cheating—but it's so awesome, I can't leave it out. When my youngest (age seven at the time) tested it out on her breakfast toast, she murmured in total bliss, "Oh, Mom, this is gooooood." Put the topping into a shaker jar (even a large, empty cinnamon bottle) or a fancier bottle like a sifter-top shaker from a kitchen supplier. Then shake the topping over anything you'd use regular cinnamon sugar on . . . only enjoy the chocolate, too!

Choco-Breakfast Topping

⅔ C. SUGAR

3 TSP. CINNAMON

2 TBSP. COCOA

1 TSP. DRY VANILLA
(OPTIONAL; SEE NOTE)

SIFT ALL INGREDIENTS together and mix well. Add to shaker and enjoy! Shake onto buttered toast, waffles, crepes, or even white chocolate popcorn before it hardens (when using on popcorn, reduce the sugar by half). Note: Dry vanilla is a powdered form of vanilla, also known as Dry Van. Leaving it out of this recipe will affect the flavor; you'll lack a bit of the vanilla kick, obviously, but the overall flavor of the topping will still be chocolaty and good. Dry vanilla is one of those uncommon items that you may have to search for at specialty cooking/confectionary stores or online.

Research shows that 14 out of every 10 people like chocolate. —Sandra Boynton

138

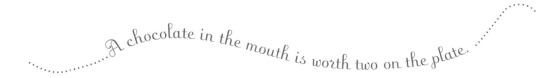

Cherry Cordial Popcorn

½ C. WATER

¼ C. BUTTER

2 C. SUGAR

½ TSP. SALT

1 CHERRY FLAVOR DRINK MIX PACKET (SUCH AS KOOL-AID)

½ C. POPCORN KERNELS, POPPED, OR 2 BAGS MICROWAVE POPCORN, POPPED

1½ C. CHOCOLATE OF YOUR CHOICE

COVER A LARGE AREA with parchment. In a medium saucepan over medium heat, combine the water, butter, sugar, and salt, stirring until dissolved. Bring the mixture to a boil and boil, uncovered, for 4 minutes. Remove from heat until it becomes still. Add the drink mix packet. Stir well until the powder is integrated. Pour the syrup over the popcorn as described in the Chocolate-Covered Popcorn recipe (p. 142): continually drizzle the syrup from the top while scooping both the popcorn and the syrup from below. Let gravity do the coating. Keep scooping syrup from the bottom of the bowl to drizzle at the top, turning the popcorn until it's well coated. Spread the popcorn onto the parchment. Melt the chocolate and drizzle over the top of the popcorn. Let the popcorn and chocolate cool and harden before breaking it into bite-size pieces and storing in an airtight container.

I'm one of those people who stock up on hot cocoa mix at the store when it's on sale because I love a hot mug of cocoa on winter mornings. (Who am I kidding? I love a mug of hot cocoa any time of year.) One of the great things about this recipe is that you can tweak it with flavorings using different creamer powders. I've found hazelnut, chocolate toffee, cinnamon, plain chocolate, French vanilla, sweet crème, almond crème, and vanilla caramel. You can probably find others. Hot Cocoa Mix is also a great idea for a gift. The recipe makes a pretty good-sized batch, so make a bit for yourself and then put some in a jar for a friend's birthday. Assuming she's a chocoholic too, she'll love you forever.

Hot Cocoa Mix

4 C. DRIED MILK POWDER

1 C. COCOA, SIFTED

2 C. POWDERED SUGAR, SIFTED

1 C. FLAVORED COFFEE CREAMER OF YOUR CHOICE

1 TSP. SALT

PUT ALL INGREDIENTS in a large bowl and mix with a big spoon, making sure to mix thoroughly. Store in an airtight container or divide into smaller airtight containers for gifts. To use the mix, add ¼ C. mix to a mug containing 1 C. hot water and stir. If desired, add some mini marshmallows and/or a squirt of whipped cream.

Exercise is a dirty word. Every time I hear it, I wash my mouth out with chocolate.

Here's a recipe that's great fun to do with the kids, especially in preparation for a movie night. Even better, it's a ball to do with a ton of variations; let each child do his or her own thing with it. See p. 139 to get a bit fancier with a cherry cordial recipe, and use that base idea to create your own new flavors. The possibilities are endless. Here's the simple version with our family's favorite embellishments.

Chocolate-Covered Popcorn

½ C. POPCORN KERNELS, POPPED, OR 2 BAGS MICROWAVE POPCORN, POPPED

1 PKG. WHITE CHOCOLATE CHIPS OR ½ LB. OTHER WHITE CHOCOLATE

1 PKG. MILK CHOCOLATE CHIPS (PREFERABLY GUITTARD) OR ½ LB. OTHER MILK CHOCOLATE

EMBELLISHMENTS AS DESIRED, SUCH AS:

MINI MARSHMALLOWS

CHOPPED NUTS (SUCH AS ALMONDS, PEANUTS, PECANS)

Ingredients continued on next page.

LAY PARCHMENT OVER A LARGE AREA on a table or countertop. Put the popped popcorn into a large bowl. Melt both chocolates in separate bowls; if you're using white chocolate chips, you may need to add a little oil or several seconds' squirt of nonstick spray to help smooth it out. It's helpful to have a second pair of hands for the next part, but not imperative: Drizzle the white chocolate over the popcorn, scooping the popcorn with a large spoon from the bottom of the bowl as you go. Don't stir, but rather continue to scoop the popcorn, bringing the chocolate and popcorn from the bottom, letting gravity do most of the work in coating the popcorn. Repeat with the milk chocolate, coating the popcorn as well as you can with the contrasting color. Spread the chocolate-covered popcorn across the parchment. Add the embellishments

Chocolate: Here today . . . Gone today!

CHOCO-BREAKFAST
TOPPING (SEE P. 138)

GOURMET GORP (SEE
P. 144)

SPRINKLES

CONTRASTING DRIZZLE
OF ANOTHER CHOCO-
LATE

while the chocolate is still wet so they'll stick. If desired, drizzle another chocolate on top and let it harden. Let the chocolate set. Break the popcorn into bite-size pieces and store in an airtight container.

*Put "eat chocolate" at the top of your list of things to do today.
That way, at least you'll get one thing done.*

You might know "gorp" as plain old trail mix, but this recipe takes the common treat to a whole new level of awesomeness. As with the chocolate popcorns (see p. 139 and p. 142), this recipe is great to make with kids; they love helping out, and each step is both easy and fun—my kids especially love shaking the powdered sugar bags!

Gourmet Gorp

2 C. POWDERED SUGAR, DIVIDED IN HALF

1 C. SEMISWEET CHOCOLATE CHIPS

¾ C. CREAMY PEANUT BUTTER

10 C. (1 12-OZ. BOX) CRISPIX OR ANY CHEX CEREAL

2 C. MINI PRETZEL TWISTS OR STICKS

1 C. RAISINS OR DRIED CRANBERRIES

1 C. ROASTED, SALTED PEANUTS OR OTHER NUTS (ALMONDS AND CASHEWS ALSO WORK WELL)

1 C. M&MS

POUR 1 C. POWDERED SUGAR into each of 2 gallon-sized zip-style bags. Set aside. In a very large microwave-safe bowl, melt the chocolate chips and peanut butter, stirring often until they are completely smooth. Add the cereal and pretzels. Stir well until completely coated. Here's where the kids come in really handy, because this part can get messy: Use a helper-buddy to hold open the gallon bags. Divide the chocolate-cereal mixture between them. Keeping a little air in the bags, seal them tightly. Now let the kids shake the bags, roll them around, and otherwise fully cover the contents in powdered sugar. Empty the bags into a big, clean bowl—preferably a shallow one to make the final mixing of the entire concoction easier. Add the remaining ingredients (raisins, nuts, and M&Ms), and mix gently. Enjoy! Variation: Use milk or white chocolate instead of semisweet.

In the cookies of life, friends are the chocolate chips.

Peanut brittle is fun, but anything is more fun if there's chocolate involved. The idea of trying to make something like this—something that involved a candy thermometer—used to make me break out in a sweat and run for the hills. Turns out it's really easy, because the candy thermometer does the work for you. This brittle isn't as hard as regular peanut brittle (where you practically break off a tooth trying to eat it). Top it with toffee bits, chocolate chips, or chopped nuts. The best part? It's a type of chocolate that you can relish slowly, because it's not gone in a quick bite and swallow. It has to be chewed and can slowly melt in your mouth.

Chocolate Toffee Brittle

¼ C. COCOA

½ TSP. BAKING SODA

½ C. LIGHT CORN SYRUP

¼ C. WHIPPING CREAM

1 TBSP. BUTTER

1 C. SUGAR

½ C. TOFFEE PIECES

OTHER EMBELLISH-MENTS, SUCH AS ½ C. MILK CHOCOLATE CHIPS AND/OR ½ C. CHOPPED NUTS

LIGHTLY BUTTER A FOIL-LINED COOKIE SHEET; set aside. In a small bowl, mix the cocoa and baking soda. Set aside. In a medium saucepan with a heavy bottom, combine the corn syrup, whipping cream, butter, and sugar. Stir over medium-high heat, mixing so the sugar dissolves. When the mixture comes to a boil, clip a candy thermometer to the side of the pan, making sure the bulb doesn't touch the bottom of the pan. Let the mixture boil without stirring until the temperature reaches 240 degrees. Remove from heat and remove the thermometer. Mix in the cocoa mixture and then pour over the buttered foil. Spread out into a rectangle with a wooden spoon to about ¼-inch thickness. The brittle will start to set quickly, so immediately sprinkle any embellishments over the top: the toffee bits, any chocolate chips or nuts, and so on. Allow the brittle to cool to room temperature. If you use chocolate chips, they'll harden last. Break into small pieces by hand and store in an airtight container.

I'm amazed when I show up with chocolate mints or suckers at an event or send them home as a birthday party treat and people are impressed. I almost feel guilty because of how ridiculously easy they are. All you really need to know is how to melt chocolate—and you've read that section right? Right. We've wowed school teachers with molded chocolate as Christmas gifts . . . gifts the kids did themselves. Each teacher gets blown away. (By the way, Mrs. B, my 9-year-old made your gift that year.)

Mints & Suckers

FOR CHOCOLATE MINTS, YOU'LL NEED:

CHOCOLATE MOLDS OF YOUR CHOICE (AVAILABLE ONLINE OR AT CANDY SUPPLY RETAILERS)

CHOCOLATE

POSSIBLY A LITTLE OIL, DEPENDING ON THE FAT CONTENT OF THE CHOCOLATE YOU'RE USING

QUANTITY OF INGREDIENTS depends on the number of mints you want to make. Figure about 1 oz. of chocolate per mint, assuming the mint is no larger than about 1 inch by 2 inches. Plan on more chocolate if you're making larger mints. Mints tend to look better with white chocolate than brown chocolate, but consider the image you're working with. A mint of an LDS temple would look far prettier in a white mint chocolate than a brown chocolate, for example, but a teddy bear would look great in brown.

If you're doing suckers, you'll need molds that have an opening at the bottom that can hold a paper sucker stick. You can purchase sucker sticks at specialty candy stores or online.

Who says chocolate isn't a food group!

To make suckers or mints:

Use a plastic container when melting your chocolate in the microwave; plastic is flexible and easier to pour out of. You can even fill a clean squeeze bottle with melted chocolate, which makes it easier to fill the molds.

Fill each mold with just enough chocolate to barely reach the level. If you have too much, the chocolate will spread out and the sucker or mint will have "shaggy" edges. When the entire tray of mints is filled, repeatedly lift it an inch or two off the counter and drop it. Do this for a good minute or so to release any air bubbles stuck inside so they won't mar the appearance of your mints. (This is a great step for young kids to do; they love dropping the trays and watching the bubbles emerge and pop.)

If you're making suckers, slip the sticks into place now, making sure they're covered by chocolate.

If you're making lots of mints or suckers, put two trays on a cookie sheet and put the sheet into the fridge so they'll harden faster.

When they've hardened completely, turn the mold upside down and pop the chocolates right out onto a layer of paper towels. (Paper towels prevent the chocolate from picking up any condensation from the room, and prevent bloom as the chocolate warms up to room temperature.) If they won't pop out right away, they're not fully hardened. Return them to the fridge for a few more minutes.

For extra wow, package in a cellophane bag and tie with a ribbon.

Despite its therapeutic value, note that chocolate is not deductible as a medical expense.

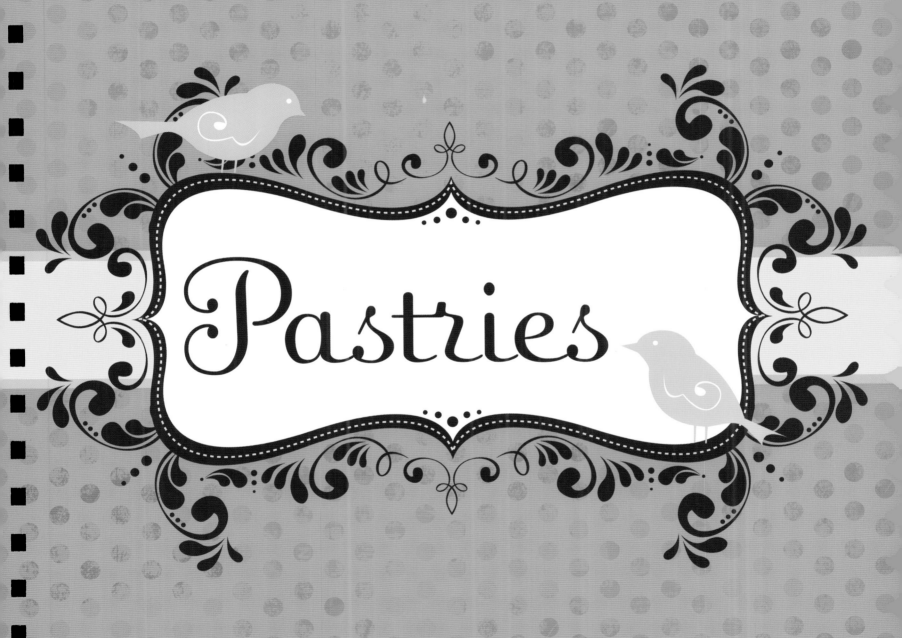

Pastries

In their simplest form, crepes are essentially very thin pancakes that are wrapped up like burritos around delicious dessert goodness, most popular in European countries. You can often find crepe appliances in the United States that make the actual cooking process much simpler (they have a domed top that you dip in the batter, and then after a few seconds of cooking, you flip the crepe to finish cooking it). I'm assuming you don't having a fancy crepe-making appliance (I don't); instead, a nice, sturdy, nonstick frying pan will do the trick.

Chocolate Crepes

1 C. FLOUR

¼ C. COCOA

3 TBSP. SUGAR

¼ TSP. SALT

1 C. MILK

⅓ C. WATER

3 EGGS

3 TBSP. BUTTER, MELTED

¼ TSP. ALMOND EXTRACT

Grease a heavy skillet or crepe pan with extra-virgin olive oil or another light oil that has a very high flash point; heat until medium hot. Meanwhile, in either a blender or food processor, blend or briefly process flour, cocoa, sugar, and salt. In a 2-cup glass measuring container, combine the milk, water, eggs, melted butter, and almond extract. While running the blender/food processor, slowly pour in the milk mixture. Process until smooth. Using a scant ¼ C., pour the thin mixture into the hot pan and immediately tilt it to spread the batter evenly into a circle, forming a thin crepe. Cook for about 30–45 seconds, until the bubbles start to settle. Turn the crepe with a plastic spatula and cook for an additional 15 seconds. Repeat until all batter is used. (You may not need to grease the skillet again or very many times.) If the crepes aren't being eaten as fast as you can make them, stack them with waxed paper or parchment in between so they don't stick to one another. If any are left over, wrap in plastic wrap. They can be refrigerated as long as two days. Makes about 12–15 crepes.

Anything tastes better dipped in chocolate.

Filling ideas:

You'll want plenty of yummy things around to fill your crepes with: whipped cream tops the list (whether regular or flavored chocolate or with a pudding), plus chocolate or caramel syrup, nuts, and even fruit like strawberries, bananas, and blueberries. Anything is game.

Filling crepes:

Place the filling down the center of the crepe, leaving about a 1-inch gap at both ends. Fold the bottom of the crepe up by an inch or two to prevent the filling from leaking out. Then roll the crepe left to right like a burrito. Garnish with additional powdered sugar or chocolate sauce if desired. Enjoy!

Biochemically, love is just like eating large amounts of chocolate.
—*John Milton*, The Devil's Advocate

You can also make regular (nonchocolate) cream puffs, which are just as good for filling with chocolaty goodness like chocolate mousse, pudding, or ice cream. But who wouldn't prefer the chocolate version? Note: Do not use the convection oven feature when baking cream puffs. In order for cream puffs to "puff," they must have steady heat rising from the bottom. A convection oven distributes heat evenly throughout an oven, which defeats the way cream puffs rise.

Chocolate Cream Puffs

1 STICK BUTTER

1 C. WATER

1 C. FLOUR

2 TBSP. COCOA

2 TBSP. SUGAR

4 EGGS

PREHEAT OVEN TO 400. Grease a cookie sheet. In a medium pan, combine butter and water. Stirring, melt the butter and bring the mixture to a boil. Add the flour, cocoa, and sugar all at once. Stir quickly over low heat until a ball forms and the mixture leaves the sides of the pan, about 1 minute. Remove from heat. Add one egg at a time, mixing each with a wooden spoon until smooth. Drop dough by heaping tablespoonfuls or through the cut-off corner of a zip-style bag. Bake for 30 minutes and let cool. Cut off a small section from the tops and remove any soft dough from the insides. Fill puffs with your choice of filling (such as White Chocolate Filling, p. 81) and replace the tops. If you can wait long enough, garnish with chocolate drizzles and powdered sugar.

A little too much chocolate is just about right.

If there's any flavor I like with chocolate better than amaretto (almond) or cinnamon, it would have to be pecan, so I decided to create a chocolate bread with pecans. At my first slice, I had to down a glass of milk—always a good sign that I've found a chocolate treat I like.

Chocolate Pecan Bread

⅔ C. SUGAR

1 STICK BUTTER

1 C. MILK AT ROOM TEMPERATURE (SEE NOTE)

2 EGGS

1 TSP. VANILLA

1½ C. FLOUR

⅓ C. COCOA

1½ TSP. BAKING POW-DER

¼ TSP. SALT

½ C. SEMISWEET CHOC-OLATE CHIPS

1 C. PECANS, CHOPPED

PREHEAT OVEN TO 350. Grease well one 9-inch loaf pan. Cream the sugar and butter. Mix in the milk, eggs, and vanilla until well combined. Add flour, cocoa, baking powder, and salt. Beat until well mixed. Add the chocolate chips and pecans and mix until just incorporated. Pour into loaf pan and bake for about one hour or until a toothpick inserted in the center comes out clean. Remove immediately from the pan (use a butter knife to loosen edges if needed) and let cool before cutting and serving. Note: Be sure the milk is at room temperature or slightly warmer, because cold milk will make the butter clump in the batter. On the other hand, you don't want hot milk, because heat can mess up how the cocoa will react, resulting in flat, dense bread that doesn't rise. I suggest either taking a cup of milk out of the fridge half an hour before making the bread or putting a cup of milk into the microwave for thirty seconds or so before adding it to the batter.

I figure if you're going to have a muffin—which you eat for breakfast while pretending it's healthy—the muffin might as well have chocolate in it.

Chocolate Muffins

2 EGGS

1 C. MILK

1 STICK BUTTER, MELTED AND COOLED

1¾ C. FLOUR

1 C. SUGAR

½ C. COCOA

2 TSP. BAKING POWDER

1 TSP. BAKING SODA

¼ TSP. SALT

PREHEAT OVEN TO 375. Line cupcake pan with paper liners or coat with nonstick spray. Beat eggs. Add milk and then the melted, cooled butter. (To help cool the butter after melting it, pour it in a plastic cup and place in the freezer for five minutes or so. The butter can be warm, but if it's hot, it'll affect the cocoa, and the muffins won't rise well.) Add the remaining ingredients; mix well. Bake for 18–20 minutes or until done. Makes 12–18 muffins.

......So much chocolate, so little time!.....

The basic recipe for these is pretty much the same as for Chocolate Cream Puffs. The biggest difference is the way you pipe them and how you fill them up. That could be tricky, but it's really not hard. As with cream puffs, you can fill them with mousse or pudding-style fillings—but unlike cream puffs, you can't fill them with sorbet or ice cream. Basically, you can't fill them with anything that you can't get out of a pastry bag (or, in our case, a plastic zip-style bag!).

Chocolate Éclairs

MAKE DOUGH as for chocolate cream puffs on p. 152.

Fill a plastic zip-style bag with the hot dough. Use scissors to cut off a corner an inch wide or slightly bigger. Pipe lengths of dough onto the cookie sheet that are roughly 3–3½ inches long and a few inches apart. There should be about 18.

Bake for 30–33 minutes. Immediately remove from the cookie sheet and cool on wire racks. Using the rounded end of a wooden spoon, poke a hole all the way through each éclair. To make more room inside for the filling, move the spoon handle around a bit into larger circles.

After the éclairs are completely cool, fill them. It's great to have a helper here holding each pastry for you as you work the filling into

Save the Earth! (It's the only planet with chocolate.)

it. Put the filling in a plastic zip-style bag and cut a small hole across the corner; if you have one, use an icing tip to help guide the filling. Have your helper "plug" the bottom hole with a finger and tell you when he/she feels the filling at the other end—sometimes it's surprising how long it takes for the filling to reach the other end, and without a helper telling you, the éclair may end up only half full.

For garnish, éclairs look extra snazzy with powdered sugar dusted over the top and chocolate syrup drizzled over that. Ridiculously easy, but eye-catching and impressive for those who think chocolate is scary and somehow a secret club. When you serve them, just nod and accept the compliments as if you're Julia Child. No need to blow your cover by telling them how little effort it took.

What use are cartridges in battle?
I always carry chocolate instead.
—George Bernard Shaw

When the going gets tough, the tough eat chocolate.

This isn't your typical banana bread. Yes, it has chocolate chips, but it's chocolate banana bread on top of that. Adding cocoa to a recipe seriously affects how the rest of the ingredients behave, so developing this recipe took a few tries to get it right, and it varies a bit from my original Chocolate Chip Banana Bread recipe (p. 164). But man, once I got it right, I got it right. It's delicious.

Double Chocolate Banana Bread

½ C. SOUR CREAM

2 TSP. BAKING SODA

1⅓ C. SUGAR

1 STICK BUTTER

2 EGGS

3–4 RIPE BANANAS

1 TSP. VANILLA

2½ C. FLOUR

⅓ C. COCOA

1 TSP. BAKING POWDER

1 TSP. SALT

1 C. CHOCOLATE CHIPS

PREHEAT OVEN TO 350. Grease the bottom of two loaf pans. In a small bowl, combine the sour cream and the baking soda. Mix well and set aside. In a large bowl, cream the sugar and butter. Add the eggs, bananas, and vanilla; mix well. Add the sour cream and soda mixture, which by now should have puffed up a bit. Add the remaining ingredients except for the chocolate chips; mix well, scraping the sides of the bowl as necessary. Add the chocolate chips and mix on low just until they're incorporated. Split the batter between the two loaf pans and bake for 55–60 minutes. Remove loaves from the pans right away and cool on racks.

Oh, divine chocolate! How I love thee.

A few years ago, I tried making zucchini muffins. When my kids heard there was some funky vegetable in the muffins, they wouldn't even taste them. But add chocolate, and wham-o! They can't get enough of my Chocolate Zucchini Bread. This is a great recipe for using all that zucchini from your garden: grate it up and freeze it in plastic zip-style bags in two-cup portions. Take one out of the freezer the night before to let it thaw, and you're good to go the next day!

Chocolate Zucchini Bread

1½ C. SUGAR

1 STICK BUTTER

2 EGGS

½ C. SOUR CREAM

1 TSP. VANILLA

2 C. ZUCCHINI, GRATED AND DRAINED (SEE NOTE)

2 TSP. BAKING SODA

1 TSP. BAKING POWDER

1 TSP. SALT

1 TSP. CINNAMON

⅓ C. COCOA

3½ C. FLOUR

1 C. CHOCOLATE CHIPS (TECHNICALLY OPTIONAL, BUT WHO ARE WE KIDDING?)

PREHEAT OVEN TO 350. Coat two 8-inch loaf pans with nonstick cooking spray. Cream sugar and butter. Add eggs and mix well. Mix in the sour cream, vanilla, and zucchini. Add all the remaining ingredients except for the chocolate chips in the order listed; mix well. Add chocolate chips and stir. Divide the batter between the two loaf pans. Bake for about an hour. Remove from pans and cool on a wire rack.

Note: If possible, grate the zucchini ahead of time and let it sit for a while so the moisture settles and drain it off; 2 cups of zucchini can yield about ¼ cup of juice to dispose of. If you can drain the zucchini before starting, your bread will turn out better. If you can't, you may need to add more flour to account for the extra moisture in the batter.

These waffles can be used for breakfast, of course, but who are we kidding? They're really a yummy dessert. Pile them with whipped cream and sliced strawberries. One wild element to the experience of eating these is that right after you take a bite, they taste like regular waffles. Then, a few seconds later, the chocolate bursts onto your taste buds like some divine reward.

Chocolate Waffles

2 EGGS

1 C. MILK

3 TBSP. OIL

1 TSP. VANILLA

1½ C. FLOUR

⅓ C. COCOA

2 TBSP. SUGAR

2 TSP. BAKING POWDER

1 TSP. SALT

IN A MEDIUM BOWL, beat eggs, milk, oil, and vanilla; set aside. In a smaller bowl, combine dry ingredients. Add to wet ingredients and stir until blended. Beat for about a minute to give the eggs a little loft. Pour the correct amount into your waffle maker and cook until the iron stops steaming. Makes about 8 small waffles. Note: For a less intense chocolate flavor (more of a milk chocolate than a semisweet), decrease the cocoa to ¼ C. and increase the sugar to 3 Tbsp.

Chocolate in the morning is good, but, honestly, it is good any time.

It took a lot of experimentation before this bread was both easy and pretty. The taste was fantastic from the very first batch, but the center looked like a meteor had hit it. My critique group loved it. "I'd buy your book just for this recipe," they said as one member grabbed a third slice. One night as I fell asleep, I figured out the (easy!) secret. When I took the next batch out of the oven and saw the beautiful tops, I literally hollered with joy and danced around the kitchen. I felt like Tom Hanks on *Castaway* after he'd created fire. Now the recipe is easy, tasty, and pretty! If I say so myself.

Marbled Chocolate Chip Pumpkin Bread

2 TSP. BAKING SODA

½ C. SOUR CREAM

1 STICK BUTTER

2½ C. SUGAR

2 EGGS

½ OF A 29-OZ. CAN PUMPKIN (ABOUT 1½ C.)

1 TSP. VANILLA

1½ TSP. SALT

1 TSP. BAKING POWDER

½ TSP. NUTMEG

1 TSP. GROUND CLOVES

4 C. FLOUR

1 C. CHOCOLATE CHIPS

Ingredients continued on next page.

PREHEAT OVEN TO 350. Grease two loaf pans. In a small bowl, combine the baking soda and sour cream. Mix together and set aside; they will react and puff up. Meanwhile, in a mixing bowl, cream the butter and sugar. Add the eggs, pumpkin, and vanilla. When they're combined, add the sour cream/soda mixture and blend. Add the salt, baking powder, nutmeg, and cloves. Gradually add the flour, scraping the sides of the bowl as necessary. Add the chocolate chips and mix just until they're incorporated. Turn off the mixer. The melted chocolate chips need to be easily pourable and thinner than chocolate chips typically are when melted, so you'll need to thin them slightly. (If you're using regular melting chocolate such as Guittard A'Peels, don't worry about this part; the melted chocolate is likely plenty runny). You can do this by adding oil (which I find messy and hard to control the amounts on) or nonstick spray, which is essentially lecithin in a can—a fantastic

You can never have too many books...or flowers...or chocolate!

1 C. MELTED CHOCO-
LATE CHIPS

SEVERAL SQUIRTS OF
NONSTICK SPRAY, AS
NEEDED (SEE INSTRUC-
TIONS)

low-fat oil that incorporates well into chocolate and that is easy to control. Just give the bowl of melted chocolate chips a 2- to 4-second spray, and stir it up. If the chocolate needs to be thinned a little more, spray a little more and mix again. When the chocolate is thin enough, pour it directly into the batter, using a rubber scraper to get it all in. Turn the mixer on low for just a couple of seconds. All you want to do is get the chocolate swirled into the batter. Even if the chocolate doesn't get fully mixed around, that's fine. You can swirl it around some more in the pans if you want to. Divide the batter between the two pans. Bake for 60–70 minutes, until a toothpick comes out clean. Cool on wire racks. Sometimes the bread cuts easier the day after baking, but you might not ever find out for sure, because it tastes so good it probably won't last that long. Tip: Since this recipe uses only half of a regular can of pumpkin, be sure to save the other half. Scoop it into a zip-style plastic bag, label it, and pop it into the freezer for later use.

*If you have melted chocolate
all over your hands,
you're not eating fast enough.*

As a newlywed, I found a banana bread recipe in a cookbook and immediately tweaked it—not because I knew what I was doing (I had no clue), but because I didn't have all the ingredients called for in the original. Now I won't make it the original way. I have friends who swear that they hate all banana bread—except mine.

Chocolate Chip Banana Bread

1¼ C. SUGAR

1 STICK BUTTER

2 EGGS

1 TSP. VANILLA

½ C. SOUR CREAM

3–4 RIPE BANANAS

2½ C. FLOUR

1 TSP. BAKING SODA

1 TSP. SALT

1 C. CHOCOLATE CHIPS

PREHEAT OVEN TO 350. Grease two loaf pans. Cream sugar and butter. Add eggs, vanilla, sour cream, and bananas. (I don't mash the bananas ahead of time; I let the beaters do it for me.) Add all remaining ingredients except the chocolate chips and mix well. Stir in the chocolate chips and mix just until they're incorporated. Put half the batter in each loaf pan. Bake for 55 minutes to 1 hour. Remove from pans immediately and cool on wire racks.

It will taste good if it's made of chocolate.

I was first introduced to classic pull-apart Monkey Bread by my mother-in-law—and it usually didn't last all that long when she made it. I decided to put my own twist on it by (of course) adding chocolate to it, effectively making an already easy, yummy dessert irresistible.

Chocolate Monkey Bread

DOUGH:

1 PKG. YEAST

¼ C. WARM WATER

1 C. MILK

¼ C. SUGAR

1 TSP. SALT

1 EGG, LIGHTLY BEATEN

4 C. FLOUR, DIVIDED

1 TBSP. OIL

TOPPING & GLAZE:

1⅓ C. SUGAR, DIVIDED

2 TBSP. CINNAMON, DIVIDED

¼ C. COCOA, DIVIDED

2 TSP. DRY VANILLA (OPTIONAL), DIVIDED

2 STICKS BUTTER, MELTED (FOR GLAZE ONLY)

COMBINE THE YEAST and warm water; mix with a fork and set aside to let the yeast activate. Combine the milk, sugar, salt, and beaten egg; add the yeast mixture and mix well. Add 2 C. flour and mix well (preferably with a machine that has a dough hook). When the dough is smooth and glossy, add the oil and mix in. Add enough remaining flour to get a dough that is not too sticky.; allow to rise for about 30 minutes. Turn dough onto a lightly floured counter and roll out to about ¼-inch thickness. Using a pizza cutter, slice the dough into 1-inch squares. In a medium bowl, sift and mix ¾ C. sugar, 3 tsp. cinnamon, 2 Tbsp. cocoa, and 1 tsp. dry vanilla. Add the dough pieces and stir to coat. Put into a Bundt pan that's coated with nonstick spray. Let rise while the oven preheats to 400 degrees. Combine melted butter with remaining sugar, cinnamon, cocoa, and dry vanilla. Pour over the top and bake for 10 minutes. Reduce heat to 350 and bake for an additional 20–25 minutes. Turn out immediately onto a plate; serve warm.

The dough is easy to make, but you have two other easy options:
—Use canned biscuits cut into quarters: 3 cans of regular-sized biscuits, not "grand" size.
—Use frozen roll dough: use about 30 thawed rolls.

165

Icings, Toppings, & Dips

The idea of chocolate fondue is dipping yummy stuff into chocolate and stuffing it into your face. Those chocolate fountains have made an art out of chocolate fondue, but while they look cool, they can't taste as good as the recipes below. To make chocolate flow in smooth sheets, though, a lot of oil has to be added. In other words, you're eating less chocolate and more fat. Yum . . . ? I prefer a simple fondue set with a fondue pot, or one of those porcelain fondue sets that has a tea light candle below it that keeps the chocolate melted. To dip the goods, use fondue forks, bamboo skewers, or even toothpicks.

Chocolate Fondues

YOU CAN DIP ALMOST ANYTHING INTO FONDUE THAT GOES WITH CHOCOLATE AND CAN BE SKEWERED, BUT HERE ARE SEVERAL POPULAR IDEAS:

POUND CAKE CHUNKS

ANGEL FOOD CAKE CHUNKS

BANANA SLICES

PINEAPPLE PIECES

APPLE SLICES

STRAWBERRIES

GRAPES

MANDARIN ORANGE WEDGES

GRAHAM CRACKERS

Ingredients continued on next page.

GENERAL FONDUE DIRECTIONS:

Melt all ingredients (preferably using the microwave method or the double-boiler method). When everything is melted smoothly and mixed, pour the mixture into the fondue container. Keep the setting on low or be sure the candle below the fondue keeps burning. Set out the items you'll be dipping onto a tray and provide everyone a fondue fork or skewer for dipping (if neither is available, use a new toothpick for each item you dip).

Classic Chocolate Fondue

1 12-OZ. PKG. SEMISWEET CHOCOLATE CHIPS

½ C. WHIPPING CREAM

2 TBSP. VANILLA

Milk Chocolate Fondue

1 12-OZ. PKG. MILK CHOCOLATE CHIPS

½ C. WHIPPING CREAM

2 TBSP. VANILLA

168

MARSHMALLOWS

CINNAMON BEARS

PRETZELS/PRETZEL STICKS

COOKIES

BITE-SIZE PIECES OF RICE CRISPY TREATS

Toblerone Fondue

3-OZ. TOBLERONE CHOCOLATE BAR

½ C. SEMISWEET CHOCOLATE CHIPS

5 LARGE MARSHMALLOWS

½ C. WHIPPING CREAM

Amaretto Fondue

1 12-OZ. PKG. MILK CHOCOLATE CHIPS

½ C. WHIPPING CREAM

1 TSP. ALMOND EXTRACT OR ¼ C. TORANI SYRUP, AMARETTO FLAVOR (AVAILABLE IN THE COOKING AISLE, OFTEN NEAR THE COFFEE FLAVORINGS)

Note: If using the Torani syrup, decrease the whipping cream slightly and/or add extra chocolate so the fondue isn't too thin.

Mint Chocolate Fondue

1 12-OZ. PKG. SEMISWEET CHOCOLATE CHIPS

½ C. WHIPPING CREAM

1 TSP. MINT EXTRACT

Symphony Fondue

½ 12-OZ. SYMPHONY CHOCOLATE BAR

½ C. SEMISWEET CHOCOLATE CHIPS

5 LARGE MARSHMALLOWS

½ C. WHIPPING CREAM

169

Classic Chocolate Buttercream Icing

1 STICK BUTTER, SOFTENED

1 TSP. VANILLA EXTRACT

DASH OF SALT (ROUGHLY ⅛ TSP.)

½ 32-OZ. BAG POWDERED SUGAR, OR ABOUT 4¼ C.

⅔ C. COCOA

5–8 TBSP. MILK, AS NEEDED

BEAT BUTTER and vanilla. In a separate bowl, sift together powdered sugar, cocoa, and salt. Add a generous ½ C. or so of the powdered sugar mixture to the butter mixture, followed by 1 Tbsp. milk. Continue alternating between the two, mixing well between each addition, until you reach the desired consistency.

Oh, okay. I guess Hershey, Pennsylvania, is not nice. A whole town that smells like chocolate—whatever!
—Doug Heffernen on the sitcom
The King of Queens *when his wife complains about never vacationing anywhere nice.*

Ganache is essentially chocolate mixed with heavy cream. The ratio of chocolate to cream varies widely, depending on the recipe, resulting in a variety of textures, thicknesses, and uses. Ganache is one of the easiest chocolate recipes to make. Even better, it looks and tastes impressive. Keep the simplicity a secret; go ahead and let your friends be impressed.

Ganache Icing

4 OZ. SEMISWEET CHOCOLATE (1 REGULAR BAKING CHOCOLATE BAR)

1 C. HEAVY CREAM

FOLLOWING THE GUIDE at the beginning of the book (see pp. 5–7), melt the chocolate until warm and smooth. Warm the cream slightly either on the stove or in the microwave so it's close to the same temperature as the chocolate. Stir the cream into the chocolate, scraping the edges and mixing thoroughly. If flecks of chocolate form, reheat the mixture slightly (perhaps only ten seconds in the microwave or over the stove). Remove from heat and continue stirring. You can pour it over a cake while the ganache is still warm, or wait for it to thicken slightly as it cools. It will harden into a glossy, impressive-looking shell. If you want a somewhat thicker icing that you can actually spread, wait for the ganache to cool completely and then beat it with a hand mixer for a few minutes to give it additional volume.

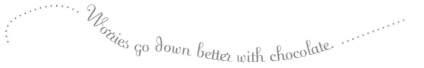
Worries go down better with chocolate.

Fudge Sauce

¼ C. COLD WATER

1 ENV. UNFLAVORED GELATIN

⅔ C. COCOA

1¼ C. SUGAR

⅛ TSP. SALT

½ C. MILK

1 STICK BUTTER, CUT INTO PIECES

2 TSP. VANILLA EXTRACT

PUT WATER IN A SMALL bowl and sprinkle gelatin on top. Set aside. In a medium saucepan, whisk cocoa, sugar, salt, and milk until smooth. Cook over medium heat, stirring constantly, until boiling. Remove from heat. Add butter and stir until the butter is fully mixed in. Add vanilla and stir. Bring to boil again. Add softened gelatin and mix until fully dissolved. Refrigerate for 2–3 hours, until the fudge sauce has thickened. Makes about 2 cups.

Chocolate ice cream is exquisite.

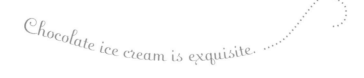

"Chocolate is a perfect food, as wholesome as it is delicious,
a beneficent restorer of exhausted power.
It is the best friend of those engaged in literary pursuits."
—Baron Justus von Liebig

Amaretto Truffle Icing

2 OZ. UNSWEETENED BAKING CHOCOLATE

½ C. SEMISWEET CHOCOLATE CHIPS OR DARK CHOCOLATE, ROUGH-CHOPPED

1 STICK BUTTER

1 TSP. ALMOND EXTRACT

⅔ C. WHIPPING CREAM

⅔ C. COCOA (OPTIONAL; SEE INSTRUCTIONS)

3–5 C. POWDERED SUGAR

IN A MEDIUM-SIZE MICROWAVE-SAFE BOWL, melt the two chocolates and the butter for about a minute. Stir. Continue to melt at 30-second intervals until almost, but not quite, liquid. Stir periodically until the retained heat melts the rest. To the chocolate mixture, add the almond extract and whipping cream. Beat on low to mix in, then switch to high for 30 seconds. Reduce speed. If using cocoa, sift it with 1 C. powdered sugar. (The cocoa will result in a darker icing. If you want a lighter chocolate icing, omit the cocoa.) Add the cocoa/powdered sugar mixture, mixing well on low speed. Gradually add more powdered sugar, beating after each addition, until you reach the desired consistency. A very stiff consistency—too thick to spread—can be used in a pastry bag to pipe truffle-style "kisses" onto the top of a cake or cupcakes, while a thinner consistency lets you spread the icing traditionally. Either way is delicious!

This easy icing can be made thinner for spreading or thicker for piping (such as onto cupcakes), depending on your preference. Since I tend to be a "go for the easy way" kind of girl, I usually spread icing, but I know a lot of people who love to pipe it because it does look pretty darn neat. If you want to pipe it, you'll need to add more powdered sugar.

Chocolate Cream Cheese Icing

1 8-OZ. PKG. CREAM CHEESE, SOFTENED

½ STICK BUTTER

1 TSP. VANILLA

½ C. COCOA

3–4 C. (OR MORE) POWDERED SUGAR, TO TASTE

CREAM THE CREAM CHEESE, butter, and vanilla until smooth. Add the cocoa and mix in well. Gradually add the powdered sugar, 1 C. at a time, until it's the desired consistency. How much powdered sugar you use will be determined by things like the humidity in your area as well as whether you want to spread or pipe the icing. Chances are if you want to spread it, you'll use around 3 C. For piping, you'll probably use an additional 1–2 C.

"According to Reader's Digest *diet tips, nuts have healthy fat. Always keep a few in your pocket to stave off hunger. So true. I like to keep my nuts wrapped in chocolate. It works every time.*
—Author Janette Rallison

This recipes goes back to my mother's penchant for doing things with whole foods—without sacrificing taste. This topping is especially good with her Mom's Read-Food Chocolate Cake (see p. 19). Yum!

Mom's Honey Chocolate-Mousse Icing

1¾ C. WHIPPING CREAM, DIVIDED

8 OZ. SEMISWEET BAKING CHOCOLATE, CHOPPED

3 TBSP. HONEY

PLACE ¼ C. CREAM in a small saucepan. Add the chocolate and the honey. Stir over low heat until the ingredients are melted and blended well. Cool, stirring every so often. (You can speed up the process considerably by putting the pan in the fridge.) In a medium to large bowl, whip the remaining cream into soft peaks. When the chocolate mixture is cool, fold it gently into the whipped cream, a third of the chocolate mixture at a time, until it's fully incorporated into the whipped cream. Spread on the cooled cake. Final important note from Mom: Enjoy licking the beaters and bowl. (Of course, Mom! I've always been an obedient child. . . .)

Chocolate and I are BFFs.

176

This thin icing is perfect for drizzling over brownies, bars, or other desserts and then letting it harden before serving. Use whatever chopped nuts are your favorites. I personally love using pecans in this recipe, but walnuts and almonds would also work well. If using almonds, consider using a bit of almond extract instead of vanilla!

Mom's Nutty Chocolate Icing

¼ C. (½ STICK) BUTTER

2 TBSP. COCOA

2½ TBSP. MILK

1 TSP. VANILLA

1½ C. POWDERED SUGAR

½ C. NUTS, CHOPPED

IN A MEDIUM SAUCEPAN, melt the butter over medium heat. Stir in the cocoa, milk, and vanilla. Heat, stirring occasionally, until the mixture begins to thicken. Remove from heat. With a whisk, gradually add the powdered sugar until it's well blended. Stir in the nuts. Immediately drizzle over brownies, bars, cake, or whatever you're icing. Store any extra in an airtight container in the refrigerator.

.... *Carpe Chocolatem* ....

Husband: Wait a minute. There were five chocolate bars in the pantry yesterday. Why is there only one today?
Wife: I must not have seen that one.

This icing is particularly good on Crooked Halo Angel Food Cake (p. 32), but it's so good that I couldn't list it just there. I've been tempted to make a batch, sit in front of a favorite movie, and just eat away. I haven't done it yet, but I'm not promising I won't.

Devilish Vanilla Icing

2¼ C. POWDERED SUGAR

¼ C. COCOA (OPTIONAL, DEPENDING HOW INTENSE YOU WANT THE CHOCOLATE FLAVOR TO BE)

1 EGG

4½ TBSP. SUGAR

2 TBSP. WATER

2 TSP. VANILLA

2 OZ. UNSWEETENED BAKING CHOCOLATE, ROUGH-CUT, OR ⅓ C. SEMISWEET CHOCOLATE CHIPS

⅔ C. BUTTER (SEE NOTE)

IN A MEDIUM BOWL, beat the powdered sugar, egg, and cocoa, if using it. Set aside. In a small saucepan, melt the sugar, water, and vanilla. Bring to a boil and boil for 1 minute. Remove the pan from the heat. Drop in the chocolate and stir, letting the retained heat melt the chocolate. Add the hot syrup mixture to the powdered sugar mixture. Beat together until mixed well. Add the butter and beat until smooth. Spread over cooled cake. Fight over who gets to lick the bowl. Note: In this recipe, shortening creates a smoother texture, while butter creates a richer flavor. Since I don't care for shortening, I use butter, but you can use the same amount of shortening.

I can't concentrate until I've had my chocolate fix.

Great for topping the Three-Layer Chocolate-Peanut Butter Bars (see p. 72) or a hundred other things, this recipe is easy and delicious for peanut butter fans.

Chocolate-Peanut Butter Icing/Filling

1½ STICKS BUTTER (¾ C.) AT ROOM TEMPERATURE

¾ C. CREAMY PEANUT BUTTER

2 TBSP. MILK

½ C. COCOA

2 C. POWDERED SUGAR

IN A SMALL MIXING BOWL, beat all ingredients together on medium until smooth. Does it get any easier than that?

Don't wreck a sublime chocolate experience by feeling guilty.
—Laura Brody, Growing Up on the Chocolate Diet

The beauty of this recipe is that it can be changed to accommodate both dark chocolate lovers and white chocolate lovers. Just beware: Either way, it's addictive, and there's a high chance that you'll be eating more of the dip than you will of the fruit you're dipping into it.

Chocolate Cherry Cheesecake Fruit Dip

16 OZ. CREAM CHEESE, SOFTENED (2 8-OZ. PKGS.)

¾ C. HEAVY WHIPPING CREAM

½ C. SUGAR

HEAPING ½ C. MINCED MARASCHINO CHERRIES (⅔ C. BEFORE MINCING)

HEAPING ½ C. CHOCOLATE, WHITE OR DARK, GRATED OR FINELY CHOPPED

2 TBSP. MARASCHINO CHERRY JUICE

½ TSP. VANILLA EXTRACT

½ TSP. ALMOND EXTRACT

BEAT ALL INGREDIENTS together on medium speed for about 2 minutes. Refrigerate. The dip keeps up to a week, but you may need to beat it again, since cherry juice tends to separate over time. Makes about 3 cups. Note #1: If grating the chocolate in the food processor, process it as briefly as possible—the friction creates heat that will melt the chocolate. It's often best to just chop the chocolate into tiny bits the old-fashioned way: use a sharp butcher knife on a cutting board with sheer muscle. Note #2: My favorite dark chocolate outside the grocery store is Peter's Burgundy. If you're serious about chocolate, it's worth finding, but it's certainly not necessary.

Everyone deserves a happy ending . . . and chocolate.
—Covenant author Michele Ashman Bell

181

Here's a recipe you'll want to mark because it has so many uses. Chocolate Glaze is quite a bit thinner than icing, and you drizzle it over whatever dessert to which you want to add a kick of chocolate, usually while the glaze is still warm. Put it on top of ice cream, pie, or cake. You can even turn plain old canned fruit into a delicious dessert by adding a delicious glaze. Best of all, it's hard to mess this one up.

Chocolate Glaze

1 C. SEMISWEET CHOCO-LATE CHIPS

2 TBSP. BUTTER

2 TBSP. LIGHT CORN SYRUP

3 TBSP. MILK

1 TSP. VANILLA

COMBINE ALL INGREDIENTS in a saucepan. Cook and stir constantly over medium-low heat until the chocolate chips are barely melted (or even when they're not completely melted and there are still a few lumps). Remove the pan from the heat. The remaining warmth from the glaze and the pan itself will continue to melt the rest of the chocolate. Stir until smooth, and use while the glaze is still warm. If there's any left over, store it in the fridge in an airtight container. Be sure to warm it up gradually (either at 30-second intervals in the microwave, stirring between them or by placing a container holding the glaze into a pan of warm water). Warning: If you reheat the glaze in a pan of water, do not let any water get into the glaze. Even a drop will mess up the chemistry of the glaze and ruin it.

Life without chocolate cake is possible, but not as worthwhile.

This syrup is great for desserts like Chocolate Crepes (p. 150), ice cream, and Chocolate Toasted Stacks (p. 64) or for breakfasts like Chocolate Waffles (p. 161), pancakes, or French toast. It's got the goodness of caramel wrapped in the wonder of chocolate. It's easy, to boot. Can't ask for more than that!

Chocolate-Caramel Syrup

1½ C. SUGAR

½ C. COCOA

¾ C. BUTTERMILK OR SOUR CREAM

1 STICK BUTTER, SOFTENED

2 TBSP. CORN SYRUP (LIGHT OR DARK)

2 TSP. VANILLA EXTRACT

IN A SMALL BOWL, mix the sugar and cocoa. In a medium saucepan, combine the sugar-cocoa mixture, buttermilk (or sour cream), butter, and corn syrup. Over medium-high heat, stir until the mixture boils. Boil for 7 minutes, stirring continuously. Remove from heat and stir in the vanilla. Serve warm on your favorite dessert or breakfast. Note #1: For a slightly thicker syrup, boil and stir longer than 7 minutes. You won't be able to tell how thick it is while it's boiling, so make the recipe once to see how thick 7 minutes will get it. The next time you make it, you can decide whether you want it thicker; if so, boil it a bit longer. Note #2: The syrup will harden when it cools completely. You can liquefy it again by warming it up slowly either in a pan (I'd suggest a double-boiler to avoid burning) or in 30-second intervals in the microwave, stirring between each run. It will still taste good reheated, but the consistency won't be quite as smooth as when fresh.

I made these when hosting book club at my house and blew away my friends. I made brownies from scratch, put a scoop of vanilla ice cream next to the brownie, and topped each dish with a chocolate-dipped strawberry that had a contrasting drizzle. No kidding—the women's mouths gaped open as if I'd rendered the Taj Mahal in cheese. At first they didn't dare bite into the strawberries, as if doing so would be tantamount to destroying the Mona Lisa, but then I admitted that my preschooler had made half of strawberries herself. Really, folks. It's that easy.

Chocolate-Dipped Strawberries

HERE'S HOW YOU DO IT: Be sure that whatever you dip will be used very soon; dipped fruit won't last long, and the chocolate will eventually start to "weep" and separate from the fruit. Before you begin, make sure that every piece of fruit is free of blemishes (you don't want to be dipping bruised or moldy strawberries) and completely dry. Hand-pat each and every piece of fruit you plan to dip with a paper towel so you can make sure each one is dry. Here's a professional secret that might gross you out: a lot of caterers don't wash the fruit they dip—they don't want to risk adding moisture that could ruin the dipped chocolate. Basic rule of thumb: Water and chocolate do not mix.

Once your strawberries are dry, set them aside and lay out parchment on your working surface. This will be where your dipped pieces will dry.

Now melt your chocolate. You can use chocolate chips with a little oil or nonstick spray added to help thin the chocolate a bit. If you have access to dipping chocolate, even better—it tends to have a much higher oil content, so it melts smoother and coats more easily. You can get similar

While there is chocolate, there is life.

results by adding more oil yourself until you reach a consistency that's easy to work with. Thick chocolate simply won't coat well—if your chocolate starts out good but then gets difficult to use, try warming it up a bit. It could be cooling off too much. If that doesn't work, add a little more oil.

The only other issue to worry about is whether your chocolate is too hot; if it is, it will harden with bloom on it—and that's just ugly. Ideally, the chocolate should be a little cooler than body temperature, around 85 degrees. If it feels too warm, stir it to cool it down. This is one way that oil can help: cool chocolate can often be thick chocolate, but added oil can keep it thin.

Holding a strawberry by the stem, gently dip it into the melted chocolate most of the way. Leave some of the red showing for visual effect. Let some of the excess chocolate drip into the bowl. Lay the strawberry on the parchment to harden. Repeat with the rest of the strawberries.

Melt a second, contrasting color of chocolate to drizzle over the top, using a plastic squeeze bottle or the zip-bag trick (see p. 7). Drizzle dark chocolate over milk, white over dark, dark over white, or other colors if you have them (pink over milk looks really pretty, for example). Some people add other embellishments—like a sprinkling of nuts—while the chocolate is still wet, but that's optional.

How many dipped strawberries you get out of a bag of chocolate chips will depend entirely on how big the strawberries are, how deeply you dip them, and how thickly you coat them with chocolate. Experiment to decide how many ounces of chocolate you need and how you like to make them.

These are solid chocolate cups you can fill with mousse, sorbet, ice cream, or holiday treats. Here's the trick: they're made by using water balloons as the mold. In spite of being surprisingly easy to make, they pack a huge visual punch for any occasion. You'll please—and impress—the crowd every time. The basic tulip cup can be tweaked a bit in the dipping process to create a bunch of other shapes that work for different holidays and occasions, so be sure to check out the variations below.

Chocolate Tulip Cups

DETERMINING HOW MUCH Chocolate You'll Need

For Tulip Cups, I prefer to use melted Guittard A'Peels—they're available at most chocolate- and candy-supply stores and come in bulk. They look like giant, flat chocolate chips (only they're better!). A lot of grocery stores (including Maceys and WalMart) sell "bark" chocolate or melting chocolate that works well. You can also use regular chocolate chips, but add a tablespoon or two of oil to get the consistency a bit thinner than regular melted chips.

To determine how much chocolate you'll need for your cups, use this guideline:

2 oz. melted chocolate = 1 tulip cup

In other words:

1 lb. Guittard A'Peels = 8 tulip cups OR

1 12-oz. bag chocolate chips = 6 tulip cups

Families are like chocolate . . . mostly sweet, sometimes with a few nuts!....

However (and that's a big, fat HOWEVER), that's in the ideal Tulip Cup world. It's unlikely you'll actually get quite that many. Plan on getting one or two fewer Tulip Cups per pound of chocolate. Inevitably, a couple of balloons will pop (splattering chocolate all over your kitchen and ruining the cup), a few cups will break in transport, or you'll suffer some other "casualty." The amount of chocolate per cup will also vary depending on the size of balloon you're using and if you're doing one of the variations below that requires more coverage than 2 oz. of chocolate.

BASIC CHOCOLATE BALLOON CUP INSTRUCTIONS

Blow up as many water balloons as you want tulip cups—plus several to spare to account for casualties—and tie them off. The ideal bottom diameter should be around 3–4 inches. Line baking sheets with parchment or waxed paper.

Melt chocolate in a glass or glazed earthenware bowl (see pp. 5–7 for instructions on melting chocolate).

Create a small "foot" for each cup by placing a dollop of melted chocolate on the parchment for each cup to sit on. Space the "feet" several inches apart so the dipped balloons won't touch. Jiggle the paper slightly to smooth the chocolate into neat puddles, each a little more than an inch across. The foot will prevent a hole from forming at the thin contact point where the balloon and the parchment meet.

Holding a balloon at the knot, dip it into the melted chocolate and rest the bottom slightly beneath the surface. Gently lean the balloon to one side. The top ¼ to ⅓ of the balloon should remain bare.

Tilt the balloon in the opposite direction, again coating to within ¼ to ⅓ of the top. You now have two tulip petals. Pull the balloon upright again and allow excess chocolate to run down for a few seconds before dipping the other two sides in the same manner. This X pattern will create four tulip petals. You can play with making three slightly wider petals instead of four. With more than four, the petal effect begins to be lost.

After fully dipping the balloon, let excess chocolate drip off, then set it directly on top of one of the "feet." It doesn't matter whether the foot puddle is hard or soft.

After dipping all of the balloons, allow the cups to fully set. (Cooling them in the fridge speeds up the process, but increases the likelihood that a few balloons will pop.)

When the chocolate cups are completely hard, gently snip each balloon near the knot. Allow the balloon to slowly deflate, leaving behind the hardened chocolate cup. Remove any balloon pieces. Store the cups in a cool, dry place until ready to use.

Hint: As you work, take care to keep the chocolate nice and warm—not hot. If the chocolate is too hot, the balloons will pop, spraying liquid chocolate everywhere. If you can comfortably handle the bowl, touch the chocolate with your bare hands, and it's still runny enough to dip in, it's about right. Ideally, the chocolate should be around 85 degrees, which is below body temperature. If it feels too warm, stir it a bit to work in some air and cool it down.

Allergy Alert: Most water balloons are made with latex plastic. While this is not a problem for most people, individuals with a latex allergy should never be served Tulip Cups. Even minimal contact with latex—such as happens with this recipe, where the chocolate has touched a latex balloon—could be enough to send an allergic person into potentially fatal anaphylactic shock.

How to Make Marbled Tulip Cups:

Marbled chocolate cups are particularly beautiful and impressive, and best of all, they're easy to do. Follow the basic instructions for Tulip Cups, but use a contrasting color of chocolate for the marbling. For example, marble dark chocolate into milk chocolate or white into pink. Drizzle a little of the contrasting color on the top of the darker chocolate. Swirl them together just a bit with a butter knife or spoon, but not until they're mixed together. Dip the cups as usual, adding more of the contrasting chocolate as needed.

Hint: When marbling, you may want to do the balloon dipping in a smaller reservoir of the main chocolate color rather than in the container you melted it in. For example, use a large soup bowl with some of the darker chocolate. Then drizzle the lighter chocolate on top of that. This avoids contaminating your primary chocolate with your secondary color.

Maybe we should give out little statues of her [on]
Mother's Day . . . made out of chocolate, and then the mothers
could take her home and bite her head off—and get a
little chocolate rush at the same time.
—Author Dean Hughes in All Moms
Go to Heaven *on the perfect and nonexistent*
ideal mother we can't live up to

191

A pavlova has a crunchy outer shell with a chewy inside that's almost like marshmallow. The story says that it's named after a famed ballerina and was invented by a chef in her honor when she came to perform in his country. Two nations—Austria and New Zealand—traditionally serve pavlovas and claim the story as their own, but according to some sources, New Zealand has the more likely claim. Serve with fresh berries, whipped cream, chocolate drizzle, or grated chocolate on top, and you've got one amazing dessert on your hands.

Chocolate Pavlova

6 EGG WHITES, REMOVED FROM THE FRIDGE 30–60 MINUTES BEFORE USE

¼ TSP. CREAM OF TARTAR

1½ C. SUGAR, SIFTED

3 TBSP. COCOA

2 TSP. CORNSTARCH

2 TSP. APPLE CIDER VINEGAR

1 TSP. VANILLA

1 OZ. SEMISWEET BAKING CHOCOLATE, MELTED

PREHEAT OVEN TO 275. In a large bowl, beat the egg whites and cream of tartar until the whites form soft peaks. Gradually beat in the sifted sugar, a few tablespoons at a time, then let the whites beat further until stiff, glossy peaks form. Sift the cocoa and cornstarch over the whites and fold in gently. Add the vinegar, vanilla, and melted chocolate and again fold in gently. Line a baking sheet with parchment. Spread the chocolate meringue mixture into a circle that's about 8 inches across. Bake in the center of the oven for an hour and a half. The outside will be crispy, and the inside will be soft. The disk will have grown and flattened. Very carefully (so you don't crack the meringue), move to a wire rack to cool completely (roughly an hour). To serve, layer the top with whipped cream. Add fruit of your choice (such as strawberries, raspberries, blueberries, kiwi, peaches, or bananas) and drizzle with melted chocolate.

The first time I heard the term *tiramisu* was in the classic scene in *Sleepless in Seattle* where it's unclear that it's simply a yummy dessert. One small problem for LDS folks: tiramisu is generally made with rum and espresso. Not exactly Word of Wisdom-friendly. This version uses different kinds of chocolate plus amaretto (almond) flavoring instead. I've been known to make it and refuse to share.

Mormon Tiramisu

FILLING:

1 PKG. WHITE CHOCO-LATE INSTANT PUD-DING

8 OZ. CREAM CHEESE, SOFTENED

¼ C. SOUR CREAM

2 TBSP. HEAVY WHIP-PING CREAM

1¼ C. SUGAR

1 TSP. ALMOND EX-TRACT

Ingredients continued on next page.

FILLING: PREPARE WHITE CHOCOLATE pudding as directed. Chill in the fridge. In a small mixing bowl, combine the cream cheese, sour cream, and 2 Tbsp. heavy cream. Gradually beat in the sugar a little at a time, allowing the crystals to dissolve in the mixture as much as possible. Add the almond extract. Remove the pudding from the fridge. Fold a small amount of pudding into the cream cheese mixture. When it's incorporated, gradually fold in the rest of the pudding until it's fully mixed together. Set aside.

Chocolate Soak: Prepare 1 C. hot cocoa at double strength (or stronger). A strong flavor like dark Belgian chocolate works well. While it's still hot, add the amaretto creamer. Stir to dissolve. Add an ice cube so it'll cool off before you assemble the dessert. Chill for a few minutes if needed.

*I have this theory that chocolate
slows down the aging process.
It might not be true, but why take the risk?*

THE CHOCOLATE SOAK:

YOUR FAVORITE HOT COCOA MIX, ENOUGH TO MAKE 1 C. AT DOUBLE STRENGTH

¼ C. AMARETTO-FLAVORED POWDERED CREAMER

1 ICE CUBE

OTHER INGREDIENTS:

6 OZ. LADY FINGERS OR 1 CAN PEPPERIDGE FARMS PIROUETTES

1 SOLID CHOCOLATE BAR

OPTIONAL GARNISHES

SLICED ALMONDS

WHIPPED CREAM

Assembling the Tiramisu: Pour the cooled hot chocolate mixture into a flat container (a pie tin works well). Dip one lady finger at a time into the mixture and line the sides of a trifle bowl or 7 x 11 glass dish. If you have enough lady fingers, you can make a prettier dessert by standing some lady fingers on end around the edges like a fence. If you're using regular lady fingers, work quickly so they don't get too soaked. If you're using Pepperidge Farms Pirouettes, let them sit a little longer to soak up more liquid. Spread half of the pudding mixture evenly on top of the soaked lady fingers layer. Grate some of the chocolate bar across the top. Sprinkle with sliced almonds, if desired. Repeat layers: lady fingers dipped in the chocolate-amaretto soak and then the cream cheese and pudding mixture. Top with more grated chocolate and almonds. Cover with plastic wrap and chill in the fridge for several hours, preferably overnight. Serve with any garnishes you wish: a dollop of whipped cream, chopped almonds, grated chocolate, and so on.

Caramels are only a fad. Chocolate is a permanent thing. —Milton Snavely Hershey

No worries here; you won't be eating chocolate with sausage, pepperoni, or anchovies. Instead, this is a dessert confection of pure chocolate joy. After you make the crust and smooth on the "sauce" (your choice of blissful chocolate icing), go ahead and let the kids help out by adding the toppings. Or make one for the kids to toss their stuff onto, and another for more grown-up toppings. Then slice up and enjoy!

Chocolate Pizza

CRUST:

1 STICK BUTTER

½ C. MILK CHOCOLATE CHIPS

1 C. SUGAR

2 EGGS

1 TSP. VANILLA

¼ TSP. BAKING POWDER

½ TSP. SALT

¾ C. FLOUR

CRUST: PREHEAT OVEN TO 350. Line a 12-inch pizza pan with foil and lightly coat with nonstick spray. Melt the butter and chocolate chips in a microwave-safe bowl, stirring at 30-second intervals until smooth. In a separate bowl, cream the sugar, eggs, and vanilla for about 2 minutes. The eggs should be pale yellow and fluffy. Add the chocolate-butter and mix in. Add the baking powder, salt, and flour and beat just until well blended. Pour the batter onto the foil-lined pan, spreading evenly with a rubber scraper. Bake 20–25 minutes, until firm in the center but not burned at the edges. After removing the pan from the oven, immediately remove the crust with the foil and let it cool on a rack without the pan under it. After the crust cools, frost with your choice of "sauce":

Chocolate Cream Cheese Icing (p. 175)

Classic Chocolate Buttercream Icing (p. 170)

Mom's Nutty Chocolate Icing (p. 177)

Ganache Icing (p. 171) OR

2 C. chocolate-flavored ice cream

Top with a few of your favorite items from the following list (or come up with your own). Three or four is generally plenty per pizza; no need to go completely overboard:

Chocolate chips

Peanut butter chips

Chopped nuts

Drizzles of Chocolate Glaze (p. 182)

M&Ms

Nerds

Skittles

Mini marshmallows

Colorful sprinkles

Shredded coconut

Dried fruit, such as Craisins, dried blueberries, or pineapple pieces

Fresh fruit, such as sliced bananas, strawberries, and kiwi

Toffee bits (Heath brand, available in bags next to chocolate chips)

Chopped Andes mints

Squirts of whipped cream from a can

Tip: When using fresh fruit, be sure to add it right before serving so it doesn't get mushy, and don't freeze it ahead of time. Also, when using any fruit that browns when exposed to oxygen (like bananas or apples), toss it in a bowl of water with a few tablespoons of lemon juice. The lemon juice will help delay the browning effect for hours, if not days.

I give my sister Mel the credit for coming up with this amazingly cool idea. We sisters just showed up one day for our annual gift-making day, and she showed us what she'd come up with. Wow. Once again, she blew us away with her creativity—but once again, when we took a look at what she'd done, it was really a simple concept: boxes made of graham crackers held together with royal icing, dipped in chocolate, and filled with three gourmet pretzel rods each. We wrapped them in cellophane and tied them with a bow. I don't think I've ever been more popular with my friends.

Chocolate-Dipped Boxes

IF YOU'RE MAKING CHOCOLATE BOXES, YOU'LL PROBABLY WANT TO MAKE SEVERAL AT A TIME; EACH WILL REQUIRE:

2½ GRAHAM CRACKERS

2–3 TBSP. ROYAL ICING (P. 199)

MELTED CHOCOLATE OF YOUR CHOICE (SEE NOTE ON P. 199)

THIS IS A TWO-DAY PROJECT. Day One: Create the box bases. Break the graham crackers in half. Use half a graham cracker for each base and for each wall (a total of 5 halves). Use royal icing to "glue" the sides of the box to the base. A pastry bag with a tip is easiest, but you can use the zip-bag trick (see p. 7) in a pinch. The thicker the royal icing the easier this is, because it'll dry faster and the boxes will hold up rather than collapse as you make them. Let the boxes dry overnight.

Day Two: Cover a large area with parchment where you can dry the boxes once they're covered in chocolate so they have room to dry and harden. In a very large bowl, melt the chocolate at a very low temperature (I like to use an earthenware bowl at about 180 degrees; it needs to be cool enough so you can still handle the bowl with your hands). When the chocolate is fully melted (add oil to thin it, if needed), use a ladle to help dip each box into the chocolate. Use the ladle or a spoon to scoop more chocolate to cover the entire surface area of each box, inside and out. Let excess chocolate drip off, scraping some into the bowl as you go. Set each chocolate-covered box, base down, onto the parchment. Allow the boxes to set completely before touching them. Fill with treats of your choice. Gourmet pretzel rods look fantastic inside, but you can fill them with any kind of treat and wrap them with cellophane and a ribbon.

ROYAL ICING:

3 EGG WHITES

1 PKG. POWDERED SUGAR, SIFTED

½ TSP. CREAM OF TARTAR

1 TSP. VANILLA (OPTIONAL)

In a large mixing bowl, combine egg whites, powdered sugar, and cream of tartar. Beat on high speed for 7–10 minutes, until very thick. Use in a pastry bag with a tip or use the zip-bag trick (see p. 7) to make lines of icing to glue the pieces of graham cracker together. If any icing is waiting to be used in the bowl, cover with a damp paper towel, as it hardens quickly.

Variation: For a particularly spectacular-looking gift, create an extra large box by making more than one box at a time using the same concept: just use the royal icing to glue several compartments together. Mel once made a 4 x 3 box with this method; she dipped the entire thing in chocolate, then filled each section with a different treat, such as nuts, chocolates, and dipped strawberries. The final stunning result was a special Christmas gift for a family member's employer, and it definitely impressed the recipient.

Note: Semisweet chocolate looks really good on the boxes since it's darker, and it also tends to disguise blemishes and any spots that might not have gotten as much chocolate on them. This is one recipe where you'll be using a lot of chocolate, so it might be worth either buying chocolate chips in bulk and thinning them with oil or getting actual melting chocolate like Guittard A'Peels, which have a higher fat content and are made for melting.

199

Non-Edible Chocolate Bliss

One of my favorite things to do is take a long bath with a candle offering just a little light. Naturally, if you add chocolate to the experience, it's even better. Chocolate body scrubs really are chocolate: they use actual cocoa and natural oils. They're great for exfoliating with a loofah, although I've been known to head for the chocolate after I dry off. Be sure to keep the scrub in an airtight container so bathroom steam doesn't spoil it. Since the scrubs are heavy, you may need to rinse the remaining scrub down the drain after you've emptied the tub.

Body Scrubs

IMPORTANT NOTES ON BODY SCRUB RECIPES: Make these for gifts or keep them for yourself. They make up fast and easy. Once you have the basic idea of how to create a body scrub, you can play with the scents and oils to your heart's content—within the guidelines below.

Scented Oils

Do not use extracts (such as orange extract) in place of the scented oils, because extracts irritate the skin. Use oils. They are generally available at health-food stores in the cosmetics or aromatherapy sections. If you use an extract, instead of having a luxurious, exfoliating bath experience, you'll end up with irritated skin. The suggested amounts of essential oil drops are suggestions only; use more or less according to whatever you like. They're usually pretty strong, so you won't be measuring in teaspoons but in drops.

If I could, I would bathe in chocolate..........

202

Separation

Since these are natural scrubs (we aren't making them with artificial ingredients that keep everything nicely mixed together), the oils can separate from the dry ingredients somewhat between uses. Expect that and keep a spoon handy to stir it up with; use the same spoon to scoop some out for each use. (If you're giving it away, tie a little wooden spoon to the container!) Most of the recipes make about 3 C. of scrub. You can divide it into 1-cup portions for gifts, but since the scrub does separate, plan to divide it up into separate containers immediately after you make it so each gift has the same proportions.

Spoiling

If you won't be using up the scrub in a month or two, it's not a bad idea to keep it in the fridge—because, again, we aren't using artificial ingredients, and therefore we aren't using preservatives, either. While oils generally can sit on a shelf for months, a bathroom tends to have more heat and humidity than your average kitchen shelf. Heat and humidity speed the spoiling process. (Maybe that'll be an incentive to treat yourself to a bath more often!)

Salt

You can often find sea salt at health-food stores, but I've also found it at warehouse stores like Costco. It's not hard to find. You definitely don't want to use regular table salt.

Ahhhhh . . .

The scrubs are meant for use on your body more than on your face (they may be too harsh for delicate facial skin). After rubbing the scrub over your body—especially on your feet . . . oh, the heaven—the oil will leave your skin soft, so there's no need to use lotion afterward!

Ready? Let's make some chocolate body scrubs!

Specific recipes on next two pages.

Love is like swallowing hot chocolate before it has cooled off. It takes you by surprise at first, but keeps you warm for a long time.
—Anonymous

Chocolate-Orange Body Scrub

½ C. SEA SALT

1 C. SUGAR

½ C. BAKING SODA

½ C. COCOA

½ C. CANOLA OIL

8 DROPS ORANGE OIL

IMPORTANT NOTE: Before beginning, read the notes on body scrubs on pp. 202–203. In a medium mixing bowl, combine the salt, sugar, and baking soda. Sift the cocoa into the mixture and stir all dry ingredients together. In a separate container, combine the canola oil and the orange oil drops. Pour the oil mixture over the dry ingredients. Mix well, kneading if necessary to make sure the scrub is fully blended. Scoop into an airtight container.

Do you think I could bathe in hot chocolate?

204

Praline-Chocolate Body Scrub

½ C. SEA SALT

1 C. BROWN SUGAR

½ C. BAKING SODA

½ C. COCOA, SIFTED

1 TBSP. DRY VANILLA (OPTIONAL, BUT ADDS A NICE KICK OF SCENT; AVAILABLE AT SPECIALTY COOKING STORES)

½ C. ALMOND OIL (AVAILABLE IN THE COOKING SECTION OF HEALTH-FOOD STORES)

IMPORTANT NOTE: BEFORE BEGINNING, read the notes on body scrubs on pp. 202–203. Combine salt, brown sugar, baking soda, sifted cocoa, and dry vanilla (if using). Mix well. Pour the almond oil over the top and mix in thoroughly. Store in an airtight container. Stir before each use.

Chemically speaking, chocolate really is the world's perfect food.
—Michael Levine, nutrition researcher

This is definitely for children who are old enough to grasp that while the dough they're shaping looks and smells like chocolate, they shouldn't be eating it. The recipe isn't toxic, but it sure doesn't taste good—and considering it's made with a lot of salt, it might give them a tummy ache. Note: This recipe is one of the few in the book that may require a trip to a specialty confectionery store, whether brick-and-mortar or online. Chocolate flavoring (artificial or natural) and brown food coloring aren't easy to find at typical grocery stores.

Chocolate-Scented Play Dough

1 C. FLOUR

¼ C. SALT

1 TSP. OIL

2 TSP. CREAM OF TAR-TAR

1 C. WATER

2 TSP. CHOCOLATE EXTRACT OR ARTIFICIAL CHOCOLATE FLAVOR-ING

BROWN FOOD COLOR-ING, AMOUNT DESIRED (I USED AMERICOLOR CHOCOLATE BROWN, #104)

IN A MEDIUM OR LARGE SAUCEPAN, combine all ingredients except brown food coloring; cook, stirring constantly, over medium heat. Add the coloring, stirring between additions, until it reaches the shade you want. (Five good squirts turned out to be about right for me—anything less looked pinkish or light brown, not chocolate enough.) Keep stirring until the mixture is smooth and the dough pulls away from the sides into a ball. At first it will look like a big, gloppy mess—keep going. It will smooth out. Remove from heat. Flatten the dough slightly on parchment or foil so it can cool enough to touch comfortably. Knead until the dough is soft and elastic. Store in a sealed, plastic container or a zip-style bag in the fridge. The dough will stay good for months if kept clean.

Not only is this recipe fast and easy, but it's got real chocolate in it (none of that fake artificial-flavored chocolate icky lip gloss stuff that never tastes like chocolate . . . and is worse than carob!). One of the best parts is that the gloss is pretty when worn. It has a nice sheen, and the milk chocolate version is perfect for young girls because the color is subtle (and something I'd wear, for that matter). Some of the fun is experimenting with different colors of chocolate chips to find new shades. Makes a great favor for preteen birthday parties, especially since the recipe can be quadrupled while maintaining the quality.

Chocolate Lip Gloss

2 TSP. PETROLEUM JELLY

⅛ TSP. HONEY

5 CHOCOLATE CHIPS (MILK CHOCOLATE FOR A LIGHT COLOR; SEMI-SWEET FOR A DARKER COLOR)

⅛ TSP. SHORTENING

IN A MICROWAVE-SAFE CONTAINER, Combine all ingredients; microwave, uncovered, for 20 seconds. Stir. Repeat, melting at 20-second intervals, stirring each time, until chips are fully melted and the mixture is fully mixed together. Scoop into a small lip gloss or other container and freeze for 15 minutes, until completely cooled and solid. Apply to your lips! Makes about 1 Tbsp. gloss.

To quadruple the recipe, use the following:
8 tsp. petroleum jelly
½ tsp. honey
20 chocolate chips
½ tsp. shortening

A friend and chocolate is what the heart needs all the time.

Bumping It Up a Notch: Resources for Finding Fancier Ingredients

Feel like trying the bigger and better ingredients that aren't necessarily available at your local grocery store? Here are a few websites and stores where you can start your search. Do a search online for stores in your area that specialize in chocolate and candy. Look for chocolate classes, which are often sponsored by stores where you can then buy more product. Remember: This list is just a starting point.

ALISON'S PANTRY
Look at the product catalog under "Baking" for Guittard products, including bulk chocolate and A'Peels melting chocolate. Located in Pleasant Grove, Utah. http://alisonspantry.com

BAKER'S CASH AND CARRY
A simple warehouse-type store that carries a lot of supplies, including some high-end brands like Callebaut. Not all of their products are available directly from their website, but I imagine customers can call to place orders. They are located in Salt Lake City.
http://bakerscandc.web-ctr.net/

ORSON GYGI
This specialty cooking store in Utah probably has the biggest selection in Utah, whether it's for candy, chocolate, or anything else. They offer classes as well. You can find Dry Van, caramel bricks, any kind of flavoring, emulsion, candy color—you name it. Their chocolate brands include Callebaut, Ambrosia, Guittard, Ghirardelli, Peter's, NorPro, and more. http://gygi.com

Glossary

Baking Chocolate: Chocolate that comes in bars or cubes, usually unsweetened; you melt it and then add it to a recipe. Bars are usually four ounces with eight pieces; the boxes of cubes will contain eight one-ounce cubes. Be sure you read the labels and know how many ounces you're getting and using.

Baking Powder: A powdered leavening (rising) agent that helps baked goods get nice and fluffy. Similar to but not to be confused with *baking soda;* baking powder has more acid in it than baking soda has.

Baking Soda: A powdered leavening (rising) agent that helps baked goods get nice and fluffy. Similar to but not to be confused with *baking powder.* Some recipes call for both, and others will ask you to activate the soda by putting it into an acidic substance such as sour cream to start the release of carbon dioxide so the recipe will rise better. Don't neglect that step, or you'll regret it.

Bloom, Chocolate: The gray spots or cloudiness on the surface of chocolate when cocoa butter and/or sugar crystals separate from the rest of the chocolate and come to the surface. Bloom occurs when chocolate is improperly tempered or improperly stored. You can use bloomed chocolate, as the taste and texture will be only slightly affected, if at all, but the final product won't look nearly as nice. Prevent chocolate bloom by storing chocolate in a cool, dry place and not letting it undergo rapid temperature changes. Avoid bloom when melting chocolate by making sure it's not too hot and by stirring frequently so that it gets tempered well.

Boil: Cooking liquid in a pot on the stove to a temperature at which large bubbles continuously break through the surface. Not to be confused with *simmer.*

Brown Sugar: A sugar that contains some molasses, resulting in a darker color. (Light brown sugar has about 3.5 percent molasses, while dark brown sugar has nearly twice that.) When measuring brown sugar, pack it as tightly as you can into the measuring cup. This is exactly the opposite of how you should measure regular sugar (or anything else, for that matter).

Carga: The equivalent of 24,000 cacao beans, which were used as currency and even for paying taxes during the Aztec period (according to Qzina Specialty Foods). The province of Cihnatlan paid 800 cargas to the king every six months. That's nearly 38.5 million cacao beans a year!

Candy Color: A confectionary coloring used to tint candy and—for our purposes here—chocolate. Never use food coloring, professional or otherwise, for tinting chocolate. Always use candy color.

Candy Thermometer: A handy, inexpensive tool that clips right to the edge of your heavy-bottomed pot where your sugary syrup is boiling. It tells you how hot the syrup is so you'll know when to remove it from the heat for divinity, brittle, and any other candy-related recipes. Be sure to keep the bulb of the thermometer off the bottom of the pan and watch the temperature as it climbs—which it will quickly at the end—so the syrup doesn't burn.

Chocolate Boxey: Dating back to at least 1894, this term developed from the sweet, sentimental, and romantic illustrations that used to be a regular feature on boxed chocolates. In fact, the very first box of chocolates (created in 1868) had a picture

211

of Cadbury's daughter with a kitten. *Chocolate boxey* eventually came to mean anything overly romantic, idealistic, or made to look better than it is. Even people could be described as "chocolate boxey."

Coat: To cover something completely with a liquid substance, such as flavored syrup over popcorn or melted chocolate over pretzel rods.

Cocoa Bean: The raw source of all chocolate products. After harvesting from pods, the cocoa (or cacao) bean is dried, fermented, roasted, and ground to produce chocolate liquor and eventually cocoa powder and cocoa butter, from which chocolate is made.

Cocoa Butter: One of the two main products derived from the cocoa bean and eventually from chocolate liquor, the other being cocoa powder. It's the main fat content of chocolate, often added to decrease viscosity. Cocoa butter is also the main ingredient in white chocolate.

Cocoa, Dutch-processed: Dutch or Dutched cocoa has nothing to do with the Netherlands, tulips, or windmills. Instead, it refers to a process some cocoa powder goes through when alkali is added to it. The resulting color is usually more intense, and the flavor is milder. Dutched cocoa is not better or worse than plain chocolate; it's just different. You'll notice that a lot of store-bought cocoa is Dutched simply because it's a popular variation of an old favorite. Because the pH has been altered, Dutched cocoa doesn't always react the same way in recipes, so none of the recipes in this book use it.

Cocoa Pod: The source of cocoa beans, cocoa pods are between 4 and 13 inches long. They grow on cacao trees that grow up to 8 meters (26 feet) tall. Pods can start out as white, green, or red, and ripen to green, yellow, red, or purple. Each pod contains only 20–60 cocoa beans. With all the steps involved, chocolate production is time-consuming. It doesn't help that one cocoa bean doesn't go very far—consider that it can take as many as 150 beans (about three pods) to make one 8-ounce chocolate bar!

Cocoa Powder: One of the two main products derived from the fermented chocolate liquor put under intense pressure, the other being cocoa butter. Sometimes the powder is Dutched. *(See Cocoa Powder, Dutch-processed.)*

Cocoa, Unsweetened: The result of squeezing the cocoa butter out of the chocolate liquor, leaving just the cocoa behind and not adding anything to it. All recipes in this book use unsweetened cocoa powder.

Coconut Oil: A healthy oil (for your body as well as your skin) used in several recipes, which can also be substituted in several others. It bakes very well and has a very mild flavor. Found in health-food stores in the cooking oil section. It is white and remains soft but solid at room temperature (much like butter) but melts easily.

Coffee Creamers: Powders used in recipes as additions; available in a variety of flavors, including cinnamon, vanilla, and hazelnut. Also available in liquid form, but all recipes in this book use the powdered form.

Conche: A process in chocolate-making where chocolate ingredients are agitated for many hours, often for days. The longer the conching, the smoother the texture and the flavor. Many people assume that chocolate made in the United States has wax added to it. In reality, it doesn't (read the labels). Our factories are just lazy and don't conche as long as they should for a really good chocolate. The longer a factory conches, the better the chocolate.

Dark Chocolate: Chocolate with more than 50 percent of its content from the cocoa bean, which includes both cocoa powder and cocoa butter. Contrary to popular belief, dark chocolate doesn't have to taste bitter. A lot of bitter dark chocolates are a result of the soil they were grown in, how they were fermented, how long they were conched, and other factors.

Double-Boiler: A pot on the bottom boils water, and a smaller pot or bowl is placed on top to hold the chocolate; with this method, the chocolate is exposed to the steam, but not the direct heat, so it is less likely to seize. You can buy fancy double-boilers or just cobble one together with what you have at home.

Drizzle: An embellishment where a contrasting color of melted chocolate tops a project in several small, thin lines close to-gether, such as a narrow zigzag pattern. Generally done with the zip-bag trick (see p. 7) or a squeeze bottle.

Dry Van/Dry Vanilla: A white, powdered form of vanilla used in situations where the end result must be dry rather than wet, such as Choco-Breakfast Topping (see p. 138) or Praline Chocolate Body Scrub (see p. 205). Dry vanilla is usually available only at specialty stores.

Dust: Giving a light covering of powdered sugar and/or cocoa over a dessert (such as a cake or crème puff) by putting the covering into a sieve and then lightly tapping the edge with a butter knife.

Eggs: Buy large eggs only. If possible, take them out of the fridge 15–30 minutes before using them.

Eggs, Separated: To separate eggs, crack as usual, then carefully pull the two sides of the shell apart. Over a small bowl, move the yolk back and forth between the shell halves, letting the white fall into the bowl. When the white is gone, put the yolk into the second bowl. Avoid separating eggs over the bowl you'll be using either the yolks or the whites in, because the one time you think you won't pierce a yolk and make a mess of it, you will.

Egg Whites: Beating egg whites, especially for something like meringue, is best done with clean whites (absolutely no yolk), clean beaters and bowl (absolutely no trace of grease or water), and room-temperature eggs (take them out of the fridge early if you can). Beat them on high. Be careful not to let them beat so much they dry out, but beat them enough that they get stiff peaks or as much as the recipe specifies. Follow the instructions, whether it's to add sugar gradually, mix in cream of tartar (which helps keep the loft), or gently fold in other ingredients. While egg whites can feel tricky, don't be scared of them. Follow a few simple rules, and you'll be their master.

Flavoring Emulsion: A concentrated flavoring used for syrups and other confections. These are much stronger than flavored extracts from the grocery store.

Flavoring Oil: A concentrated flavoring in oil form used for syrups and other confections. Like flavoring emulsions, they're much stronger than flavored extracts from the grocery store.

Fold: A method of combining ingredients, especially when one of them is fluffy and can easily lose its loft, such as whipped cream or egg whites. Often you'll add the other ingredient in small portions at a time. Using a rubber scraper, scoop to the bottom of the bowl and roll up, "folding" the original mixture over the new one so it gets incorporated. Turn the bowl slightly and repeat until the new addition is fully mixed in. Add more of the new mixture and repeat, folding gently, until none of the new mixture is visible.

Food Color: Colorings that are not for chocolate. They are found in grocery stores and are used for syrups, icings, and many other uses, but never for chocolate.

Lecithin: Easily found bottled in health-food stores, but it is most commonly found in the nonstick cooking sprays in most people's kitchen cupboards. Lecithin works great as a chocolate thinner—just add a few-seconds' squirt to a bowl of chocolate chips you're trying to thin out, stir, and run for another 30 seconds in the microwave, then stir again.

Liquor, Chocolate: No worries; chocolate liquor has nothing to do with alcohol. It's merely the pure chocolate substance derived after the cocoa beans are collected, fermented, roasted, and ground up. Chocolate liquor is put into a press that squeezes out the cocoa butter and leaves the cocoa powder behind in hard cakes. Chocolate products are then made by recombining the cocoa butter and cocoa powder in different amounts.

Meringue: A dessert (such as Chocolate Pavlova, p. 193) or part of a dessert made primarily of sweetened, beaten egg whites, usually baked at a low temperature to dry them out rather than to really bake them. Meringue is often used to top pies or other desserts (like Pumpkin and Meringue Chocolate-Chip Bars, p. 76) or to create small embellishments to accent a dessert (like Chocolate Meringue Kisses, p. 128). Meringue is also used as the insulator for Chocolate Baked Alaska (see p. 22). For tips on making meringue, see *Egg Whites*.

Milk Chocolate: Chocolate with a cocoa bean content around 30 percent, to which sugar, milk, vanilla, lecithin, and other ingredients have been added.

Molds, Candy: *See Molds, Sucker*.

Molds, Chocolate: A plastic shape that can hold melted chocolate until set, making the chocolate into the form of the mold. Chocolate molds are available in dozens if not hundreds of styles, including many LDS shapes (such as a variety of temples). Usually one sheet (roughly the size of a standard piece of paper) has several molds in it. Chocolate molds are less rigid than sucker/hard candy ones, which can also be used for chocolate but generally cost more and aren't available in as many varieties.

Molds, Sucker: Made of hard, rigid plastic, these molds hold liquid candy until it sets into a sucker or other shape. They can also be used for chocolate molding. *See Molds, Chocolate*.

Non-pareils: Tiny embellishments used like sprinkles. They have the appearance of "seed beads."

Ounces, of Chocolate: Chocolate is often referred to in ounces rather than by volume (such as cups). In this book, I do some of both—referring to 2 ounces here or 1 cup of chocolate chips there. In general, 1 cup of unmelted chocolate is 6 ounces. You can go from there. I recommend getting an inexpensive postal scale to help measure chocolate amounts. They are easy to use and are invaluable for getting amounts right when you aren't sure how much you really need. (On the other hand, if you aren't sure how much chocolate to add, can it really hurt to throw in another handful? I mean, really?)

Parchment: A specially made paper that comes in rolls and looks much like waxed paper (but without the wax); it's used for baking. It's great for all kinds of uses, including baking cookies so they don't stick to the pan, lining cake pans, drying dipped strawberries, and so much more—without worrying about getting wax on your food. Parchment is a must for anyone working with chocolate. Look for it next to the waxed paper at your grocery store.

Pave: French for "cobblestone." Refers to square chocolates with rounded corners, reportedly one of the most popular shapes.

Phenylethylamine (good luck trying to pronounce *that* one!): A chemical related to amphetamines, phenylethylamine raises blood pressure and blood glucose levels, making an individual feel alert and content. The chemical reaction it produces in the brain is similar to the one that occurs when a person is in love, leading to its nickname, the "love drug." There is no proof that foods containing phenylethylamine (or PEA) affect PEA levels in the brain; pickled herring, cheddar cheese, and salami all have higher levels of PEA than chocolate does. Hmm. Try that on for size: "I need a pickled herring fix." Nah. We'll stick with chocolate.

Scant: Slightly less than the specified measurement. For example, a "scant half cup" is slightly less than a half cup.

Scorched/Seized: What results when chocolate has gotten too hot, resulting in a hard, lumpy, grainy mass—also known as *seized chocolate.* Scorched chocolate will no longer melt, and it doesn't even taste all that good anymore. To avoid scorching, melt your chocolate slowly, at a low heat, and stir regularly so you don't have to throw away any of your prized treasure.

Semisweet: Chocolate with at least 35 percent cacao (a combination of cocoa powder and cocoa butter). It generally has more sugar than bittersweet chocolate, although some people don't differentiate between the two.

Sift: Putting dry ingredients—especially those that tend to clump into little balls, like cocoa and powdered sugar—through a sieve or sifter to get the lumps out. Actual sifters are really handy and don't cost much (I've seen motor-powered ones for less than $20), but a sieve can do the job just fine—just fill it up and tap it with a butter knife.

Simmer: When a liquid is cooked to a temperature where tiny bubbles constantly reach the surface, especially at the edges. Not to be confused with *boil.*

Sprinkles: Small, candy-like bits sprinkled on top of unset chocolate as an embellishment. For those not using chocolate, sprinkles are also a common embellishment for cookies, donuts, cupcakes, and ice cream. They are occasionally called "jimmies." Some have speculated that the nickname is a racial slur referring to Jim Crow laws, but this theory has been proven incorrect, and the term *jimmies* is merely a fun way to refer to sprinkles.

Tablespoon: The largest of the measuring spoons. Sixteen tablespoons equal a cup, and four equal a quarter cup. In this book, the abbreviation is Tbsp.

Teaspoon: The most common of the measuring spoons. In this book, the abbreviation is tsp.

Temper: No, this doesn't refer to angry tantrums or mood swings, but when handling chocolate, it might as well, considering how testy it can behave sometimes. Tempering is the proper melting and handling process for chocolate, taking into account temperature control, aeration, and other factors. Properly tempered chocolate sets up shiny and hard, and it breaks crisply. Untempered chocolate can end up with pock marks, bloom, or a dull finish. To keep your life simple, you don't need to know the mechanics of tempering for the projects in this book. Molding chocolate and even plain old chocolate chips with a little oil added work well for all of these projects, if kept at a reasonable temperature and stirred regularly (keep them around body temperature). If you already know how to temper, you can adapt any project to your favorite chocolate.

Theobroma Cacao: The botanical name for chocolate and the tree it comes from, meaning "food of the Gods." See *Cocoa Bean.*

Vanilla Extract: One of the most common flavorings used in this book. Try to use pure extract, not the fake stuff, and use as much as recipe asks for. Don't skimp, or the results will be affected. If you have someone who has access to those huge bottles of Mexican vanilla, buy one from them—they're so good. Regular grocery store vanilla tends to be rather expensive. While warehouse memberships tend to gouge you in many areas, I've found that in chocolate baking supplies, they're surprisingly kind. Vanilla, chocolate chips, sugar, and the like are quite inexpensive. I always buy my vanilla there now, because I can get one of their jumbo bottles for far less than a much smaller bottle at the grocery store.

Vanilla, Dry: See *Dry Van.*

Viscosity: The level of friction between molecules of chocolate. The higher the viscosity, the more friction, so the less the chocolate flows when melted. Conversely, the lower the viscosity, the less friction, so the easier the chocolate pours and the more it runs. The amount of cocoa butter in the chocolate is a major factor in determining viscosity—the more cocoa butter, the lower the viscosity. Lecithin is often added to lower viscosity since it's cheaper than cocoa butter. You can also use vegetable oil or our handy version of lecithin, a couple of seconds' squirt of nonstick kitchen spray.

Waxed Paper: Cooking paper with a wax coating on one side, which you probably already have in your kitchen drawer. It's perfectly fine to use with many recipes. Note, however, that parchment tends to be better when working with chocolate—especially when you're melting things and letting them set—because wax melts. And somehow, the idea of eating wax doesn't sit well with me. Also, parchment seems to just work better for baking cookies and in other ways. I prefer it to waxed paper. They're found in the same aisle, and the cost is comparable.

White Chocolate: Chocolate is technically composed of cocoa and cocoa butter as well as any other ingredients, such as vanilla, sugar, lecithin, and so forth. White chocolate has no cocoa in it, so technically it's not really chocolate. However, high-quality white "chocolate" has at least 30 percent cocoa butter in it.

Zip-Bag Trick: An easy way to drizzle chocolate, fill éclairs, and do other nifty things with chocolate. See p. 7 for specific instructions.

Index